Engaging The Father

Sons Arise! Volume One

Mike Parsons

Engaging the Father
Sons Arise! Volume One

First published in the United Kingdom in 2023 by
The Choir Press
in conjunction with
Freedom Apostolic Ministries Ltd.

ISBN: 978-1-78963-372-6

Contents

*For the anxious longing of the creation waits eagerly
for the revealing of the sons of God...*
(Romans 8:19).

*"Arise, shine; for your light has come,
And the glory of the Lord has risen upon you"*
(Isaiah 60:1).

Introduction to Sons Arise!

Several years ago, I had an experience in which God took me out into the solar system and showed me a picture of the world spinning. As I looked, it stopped and I saw arcs of blue light all over the globe, a little like this image:

He told me that He was (and is) calling people to connect and become engaged in sonship, especially in the governmental aspect of sonship; and that these arcs were a representation of all the interactions going on around the world, interactions that I was going to connect with. At that point, I did not really know anyone around the world, so when God said "I want you to connect with people around the world," inside I was thinking "How? I don't know anybody!"

But whenever you say 'yes' to God, He finds a way. So I said 'yes' and since then this has become an outworked picture for me, as I have connected up with people across many different continents (both in person and via the internet) and in many different settings, including the six original 'Sons Arise!' conferences and intensives and the three 'Restoration of all Things' events.

This book, and the remaining volumes which are intended to make up this series, are a continuation of this outworking.

1. Sons Arise!

"'Sons Arise!' is the cry from the Father's heart to unveil, reveal, and release his children into their full and glorious identity and inheritance as mature sons of God, the Elohim, god-like ones." That is what the Father said to me.

Jesus described people as 'sons of God' and said we were to be like Him, so god-like ones. Let's be very clear – we are not God. But we are His sons, therefore we get to carry His heart, His reflection and His purposes; and to help others connect with Him and become mature in their own sonship.

We have a mountain of authority (mountains are symbols of heavenly authority) called Freedom Apostolic Resources (FAR) and our mandate is to gather, connect, impart and release. Even if we are not gathering in a physical location, but rather through the pages of a book, we are still looking to connect with one another and with others so that we can impart God's heart and then release people into their destiny.

What we are looking to impart is revelation, experiential truth, and not just information. I am going to share some of the things God has said to me but I will also be encouraging you to engage and activate, to open the eyes of your heart and your spirit, to actually engage with God for yourself so that you have a testimony of your own personal experience. Please take the time out to do that! Many guided engagements are included in this book, and you can also find them as audio files, ready to stream or download at freedomarc.org/etf-resources (or scan the QR code with your phone camera and follow the link which appears on your phone screen). These short engagements or activations are

Scan this QR code to view additional resources.

opportunities to taste and see. They may well be transformational and revelatory to you, depending on what you experience and how you experience it; but seek to make such encounters a part of your lifestyle, so that they become more than just something you once tasted. God wants us not only to engage from time to time but to live in the atmosphere of His presence, in dual realms of heaven and earth (and ultimately in multiple realms) at the same time.

What does it mean to live in dual (or multiple) realms? Hopefully by the end of this book you will have begun to experience that in some measure. We are spirit, soul and body; and while my body may be here, my spirit can be somewhere else (as can my soul). This is an aspect of learning to live as Jesus did. In John 3:13, talking to Nicodemus, He spoke of Himself being in heaven in the present tense – 'the Son of Man who is in heaven.' That is how He saw what the Father was doing all the time. It is not that the Father would give Him a list every day: He had a relationship of intimacy with the Father – and that is really what He wants us to develop, if we are willing to pursue it.

As a good friend of ours, Graham Jones, once said, "Pursuit is the evidence of desire." If we truly desire something, we will pursue it, so if we are not pursuing something in our life then maybe we do not desire it as much as we think we do. The things we really want are the things that we are pursuing. If we really want more of God, and more intimacy with God; if we want to find out who we each are as a son of God and what we are called to do in heaven and on earth, then pursuing the desire that is in our heart will release it. God blesses desire, so we need to learn how to cultivate desire for the right things.

This book is intended to help you pursue whatever it is that God is calling you to engage with. Every one of us can have continual testimonies of living our daily life with God, not just going to a church meeting or doing our Sunday bit but actually living every day in intimacy with the Father. Like Jesus, we can do the things we see the Father doing. So activations are exercises to help lead us into a lifestyle, not an end in themselves. They open up heaven, or they open up an experience of the Father heart of God within us and then we can live out from those experiences.

8

The focus of this first book in the series is 'Engaging The Father', and it is really not about what I have to say as much as about learning to engage the Father for yourself in intimacy as His son or daughter. With God there is no male and female, so whenever you read 'son' that always includes 'daughter' too. But I mostly use 'son' and 'sonship' because that is historically where the inheritance lies, and as we will see, this is primarily an issue of inheritance.

We have legislated for this *Sons Arise!* message to open up a safe place to help everyone connect with the Father and discover more of their sonship. You may not be familiar with 'legislating' in this context: it means that as His sons, we have both the authority and responsibility to use and enact the laws, statutes and ordinances of the kingdom of God to facilitate what He wants to do. I will share some of that legislation with you so that you can interact with it.

Scroll

I engaged with the Court of Kings and was given a scroll with some statements written on it, outlining what we are authorised to do in this *Sons Arise!* series. We will not do anything outside of what we are authorised to do, because that would be stepping outside the jurisdiction that we have and outside the relationship that we have with the Father. We are going to do what He wants and nothing more.

As you read these statements, I encourage you to let the words envelop you. We normally try to obtain intellectual information when we read, but our minds may not always understand cognitively. Instead, engage these statements with your spirit. The word of God is living and active (and even the letters of the words of God actually have life in themselves). They are not just words we read off a page, they are God speaking; and when God speaks, everything is made alive. When it says "the word of God is living and active", it does not mean the Bible. The Bible did not exist when those words were written. The Bible can be an aspect of how God speaks to us but it is not the only way. If the only thing we do is read the Bible, if we do not talk to Him in relationship, then we will only hear in one way, but He wants to talk to us in many different ways. One of the ways He talks to us is to say "I give you this authority," so receive it.

You are authorised to awaken sonship at a new level of relationship and responsibility.

You are authorised to call the eternal spirit hidden within My children to arise and shine.

You are authorised to call for the light of their eternal spirit to burst forth from the darkness into the glorious light of their full inheritance.

You are authorised to engage the Father's heart in the eternal now.

You are authorised to unveil, reveal and restore eternal memory, identity, relationships and destiny.

You are authorised to engage My children in the High Chancellors' Houses.

You are authorised to activate My Precepts, Statutes and Laws as the foundation of sonship.

You are authorised to open the House of Ordinances to reveal past and present purpose; to ignite passion and zeal for creation and its freedom.

You are authorised to open the Houses of Mantles, Scrolls and Commissioning to restore the callings and positions of heavenly governmental authority for My sons.

You are authorised to call forth the roles of chancellors, judges, ambassadors, magistrates, scribes, oracles, legislators, councillors, ministers, elders, lights, fragrances, harmonies, frequencies, doors, matrices, planners, architects, designers, artists and musicians.

You are authorised to call and prepare My children for their roles as sons with authority to restore their heritage and free their generational family lines and genealogies with the ministry of reconciliation.

You are authorised to unveil the call for My sons to arise and engage beyond the limitations of the imagination of this age.

You are authorised to unveil and reveal the dimensions and domains that exist beyond the limitations of earth-bound consciousness.

You are authorised to open the possibilities that exist beyond beyond, so that My sons can arise and take their places and positions within the councils and assemblies of the dimensions that are preparing the ages to come.

You are authorised to release the sound of the Father's heart, beating with the deepest desire to inspire My children to shake off the shackles of their earth-bound existence and arise as sons to the glorious liberty of their eternal destinies as co-creators.

"Sons Arise!" is the cry from the Father's heart to unveil, reveal and release His children into their full and glorious identity and inheritance as mature sons of God, the Elohim, god-like ones.

God gave me that scroll and I took it into my spirit, and now that scroll empowers, guides and directs me. Then I was able to make some decrees and declarations with the authority I had been given, to call things into being like the Father called things that were not as if they were. In His heart, in His desire, in His mind, He saw something, spoke it out, and it was so. All of us can do the same: we are all creative in our lives, and we all make choices that affect our daily lives, but are we making those choices based in our sonship or in our earthly thinking?

Declarations

I made some declarations on the basis of what was written on the scroll. Again, let your spirit respond. Even before he was born, John the Baptist leapt in Elizabeth's womb because he felt the presence of Jesus in Mary's womb; he felt the atmosphere, the frequency being emitted or released. We can do the same. When we connect with the heart of God, it will stir us and empower us and even though we might not understand it, it will begin to move us. At the time, I do not really understand 99% of the things I experience, and yet something in them moves me. Ten years ago I would have had to know, and I would have gone searching to find it, but now I have learned to just rest.

As you do begin to respond, both to these declarations and to further experiences you may have as you engage over the coming days (and even years), you may well find that the Father uncovers areas of brokenness and fragmentation within your soul which need healing and restoration. Do not resist that; go with it. I recommend you journal everything He speaks to you as He reveals His truth and heals your wounds.

I call for the awakening of sonship at a new level of relationship and responsibility.

I call the eternal spirit hidden within God's children to arise and shine.

I call for the light of the eternal spirit of God's children to burst forth from the darkness into the glorious light of their full inheritance.

I call for the opening of the veil between time and eternity to reveal the Father's heart in the eternal now.

I call for the unveiling, revealing and restoration of eternal memory, identity, relationships and destiny.

I call for the release of the sound of the Father's heart, beating with His deepest desire, to inspire God's children to shake off the shackles of their earth-bound existence and arise as sons to the glorious liberty of their eternal destinies as co-creators.

I call for an open heaven environment in which God's children can hear the cry from the Father's heart to unveil, reveal and release them into their full glorious identity and inheritance as mature sons of God, the Elohim.

I call for the gathering angels to be released to remove all obstacles and stumbling blocks from those who willingly open their hearts and minds to the light and fire of God's eyes.

I call for the sound of many waters to release the call to destiny to resonate within the hearts and minds of God's children.

I call for the hearts of God's children to be turned towards their heavenly Father for restoration of relationship and responsibility.

I call for the love bombs of heaven to explode with revelation of the depth of the Father's love for His children over the *Sons Arise!* environment.

I call for the lightning bolts of heavenly revelation to penetrate the hearts and minds of those who need the destruction of fortresses, strongholds and protection mechanisms to reveal their hidden father wounds and scars so that they can be healed.

I call for the Freedom portal to be opened and the sentinel angels to permit access to the legions of the angelic host who bear the gifts of destiny's call to sonship.

I call for an increase in the levels of power and presence so that it becomes manifested glory during this season of new intensity.

I call for the suspension of all barriers of time and space for all to experience the atmosphere during all activations and encounters under an open heaven...

Responsibility

The *Sons Arise!* mandate is to equip God's children to arise and take their places as sons in heaven and on earth, both relationally and responsibly; to equip the sons of God to manifest heaven on the earth. "Your kingdom come, Your will be done, on earth as it is in heaven" is something we have probably prayed hundreds and hundreds of times. I used to think: we pray, He does it, then we say thank you. That is what it is like for young children, but it would be strange if I were to treat my children when they are adults as I did when they were 5 years old. God expects us to mature in our sonship so that we begin to take responsibility to do some of those things – and not just the earthly but the heavenly too. If something is going to manifest on earth, it is our responsibility now to establish it in heaven. When we did not know, we were not responsible; but once we do get that revelation, we become responsible to administrate heaven on earth.

God is not just sitting on His throne, sovereignly doing it all. He has a whole entourage of the heavenly host who do things for Him, and you can read in the Bible about the different courts and assemblies of heaven in which He interacts with the angelic realm. We also are part of that arrangement, and we are 'seated in heavenly places' in positions of authority that we need to administrate so that heaven comes to the earth. Again, heaven does not just suddenly turn up on the earth: we are actually a gateway of heaven into the earth, as you will find in the story of Jacob at Bethel in Genesis 28. Heaven is supposed to manifest through us: that is why we have to be open for the rivers of living water to flow through us, as Jesus said.

I believe God wants to reveal who we are so that we can fulfil the purpose for which He created us in the first place, for relationship and responsibility (so we do not need to fear the responsibility aspect). The books in this series will build on one another, so that in the end each of us will know more of our eternal identity, our position in heaven and our governmental authority, and will be able to discover and fulfil our destiny.

Creation's cry

Ultimately our mandate and goal is to see the sons of God answer creation's cry, its groaning for freedom, by taking their multidimensional places in the heavenly realms to establish heaven on earth through new order *ekklesias* and Embassies of Heaven.

Creation is groaning at a low frequency because it is not in tune with the harmony of heaven; it is out of sync and longing for freedom. If we take our places in sonship we will answer that groan. There are multi-dimensional places that we can engage. Originally Adam and Eve were in the garden which God gave them, connected to Eden (the garden of heaven). Because they were in relationship, they could walk in both realms. God wants to restore that, so He wants places on earth that overlap with heaven – we call them *ekklesias* (we prefer not to use the word 'church,' because that conceals the meaning of the original word, 'a gathering of people around a purpose' – that is, God's purpose in relationship and responsibility).

Embassies of heaven are such places on earth that represent authority in heaven. Just as the US Embassy in Grosvenor Square in London represents the US here (and is regarded as American soil within the UK), we want heaven's soil on earth, under the laws and government of heaven. Our goal is to help people be equipped to establish those Embassies of Heaven. Anyone can do that if they have been called and mandated, and a lot more people are called and mandated to do something like that than they think. We are conditioned to assume that such things are only for experts, those who have been to Bible College, or have some sort of theology degree. Perish the thought that you would need something like that to be able to do what God is calling you to do! We are having to have our minds renewed so that we can see what God wants us to do and respond to His call, and I believe we are

15

going to see multiple expressions of these kinds of beachheads of heaven on earth in the future.

Fatherhood and sonship

We have a law, a piece of legislation, that authorises us to be a place where fatherhood and sonship can be restored and experienced, where reconciliation and restoration of relationship can take place and destiny can be discovered and fulfilled, the Law of Fatherhood and Sonship.

> I decree the law of fatherhood and sonship.

> I call forth the spirit that turns the hearts of the children back to their Father.

> I call forth a new dimension in intimacy and relationship in sonship.

> I call forth the alignment in the spirit with the 4 faces of God: Lion, Ox, Eagle, Man.

> I decree new foundational government to be established by resonating with the sound frequency of heaven that is calling for restoration.

> I decree new kingdom government and a new season in which lords rise up, take their heavenly positions and responsibilities, and establish the new.

Legislation decrees for Sons Arise!

> I call upon the Father to open our hearts and minds to see blind-self areas of independence where our souls' needs for affirmation are being met outside of the true love within the relationship of I AM.

> I call for the light to shine into this darkness to reveal the hidden motives of our hearts.

I call for the Law of Removal of Religious Restrictions to be enacted to lift the veils of blindness off the eyes of all engaging and connecting with this teaching.

I call upon You, Jesus, as our husband to demonstrate Your true love for us and reveal the true nature of our salvation, reconciliation, restoration and redemption from our fallen, lost state of identity; and unveil the way, truth and the life to us by bringing us into the Father's arms of love.

I call on You, Father, as the lover of our souls, to reveal Your true essence in deeper love, to take us to a new level of experiencing Your true nature and character and to draw all of us into Your heart of love.

I call upon You, Father, to open up eternity to all Your children here to know themselves at a deeper level as they gaze at the mirror of Your smiling face, look deep into Your eyes and experience love's consuming, passionate fire.

I call upon You, Father, to draw us deeper into Your love and to call from deep within Your true essence to the deepest parts of our fragmented souls to reach the most traumatised, separated and fearful parts of us, drawing them into wholeness and sonship.

I call upon You, as our loving Father, to expose and reveal all our protection, defence and coping mechanisms. Reveal all the barriers and walls that have imprisoned us and smash, tear down and demolish all that separates us from Your love and our true identity as Your sons.

I call upon You, as our loving Father, to heal our brokenness by pouring out love's lavish, rich, healing oil and releasing the sounds, fragrances and frequencies of Your power and presence to bring us into the true rest of wholeness and peace.

I call upon You, Father, to reveal the adoption into Your family to all of our fragmented souls' broken parts,

17

welcoming them to be reintegrated and restored back to the oneness of our origin within Your heart.

I call upon You, Father, to restore us, Your children, to the image of our true sonship; to reconnect us with Your original desires, thoughts and intentions for our sonship and its destiny.

I call upon You, Father, Son and Holy Spirit, to deliver us from our orphan spirits and welcome us deeper within the circle of Your love to dance with You, the lover of our souls.

I call upon You, Father, to affirm us as Your beloved sons; cocoon us within Your amazing love for us and, as our Dad, reveal the height, breadth, length and depth of Your love dimensionally in heaven and on earth.

I thank you for being the best Dad in the whole universe, for being all that we could ever want or need.

I thank you for being lavish, abundantly overflowing with new covenant love, joy, peace, patience, kindness, goodness, faithfulness and gentleness.

2. Engage in the Earth Realm

The true nature of God

Through the intimacy of a deeper relationship with the Father we will embrace our destinies as sons: to answer the groan of all creation by revealing the true nature of God and the true essence of love expressed in our glorious freedom.

It is a huge thing that God is doing around the earth, revealing Himself as He really is, in contrast to how religious systems have portrayed Him. He is nothing like I thought He was. He is nothing like I thought He was even when I first began to experience Him, because those early experiences were still conditioned by my thinking. Only when He deconstructed my thinking and revealed Himself could I realise that He is so much better than I ever thought; that I can totally trust Him; that He is intrinsically Love. If it is not love, it is not God; and love is the plumb line which we need to measure everything against, because God is love.

That love has to be experienced, it cannot be theoretical. We need to experience love in order to live from that place of love.

Sonship

We are all children of God who have an inheritance and are training in the family business. As sons, we are included in the divine circle of relationship that is Father, Son and Spirit, reconnected to the true reality of God's original intention for our identity and destiny.

Yet we cannot be recognised as sons until we recognise that we have a Father. That is why we have a generation struggling in their identity today: they are fatherless. So many children do not have a father at all, and many have a father who is absent in one way or another. So we need to have a new level of relationship with the Father if we are going to be sons.

- Sonship is a state of being included in the circle of relationship that is Father, Son and Spirit.
- Sonship is the state of being reconnected to the true reality of God's original intention for our identity and destiny.

This is not a matter of theory, but of experience we gain through practice. We will need to go:

- Deeper into intimacy with God
- Deeper into God Himself
- Deeper into the Truth – Jesus
- Deeper into revelation
- Higher into the creative light realms of heaven, into creative light
- Into the heart and mind of God outside of time and space.

Encounters

The first time I went into the heart of God outside of time and space, my mind got fried. I just could not relate to it because everything is 'now' with God, whereas everything in our life has been linear. But once I went in with the attitude "I am not going to try to figure this out, I am just going to absorb it, receive it into my spirit and allow it to unveil the truth in my spirit," then I had many powerful encounters that I had never dreamed or imagined possible, just by being in His heart. You may be wondering, "How can I do that?" We will do some activations to help you.

Forerunners go somewhere and say "Hey, it's great over here, why don't you come on over?" Everything I am describing to you is my own experience, not theory. I am sharing with you what I have been able to engage; and if I have been able to engage it, coming from my scientific, analytical background and my church history, I believe anyone can. All we need is a little bit of help to begin to get on the journey and to see the door open.

God is calling His children, His sons, to come out of the wilderness. He is calling His sons to cross over into their supernatural inheritance beyond the veil. The veil is torn open for us to come into a different realm, into a different dimension of our relationship with God, and into the realm of heaven itself. Religion will tell you that you cannot go into heaven until you die (or at least have a near-death experience). It is just not true. I have been to heaven. I have met Enoch in heaven. The Bible is full of people who went to heaven: John, Ezekiel, Joshua the High Priest – and Moses and the seventy elders had a meal with God on a sapphire pavement. If you have chosen to read this book, you may well already know this, and may be ready to engage in heaven yourself.

He is calling His sons into deeper levels of intimacy, calling us all to know Him by experience, not intellect. That does not mean you have to throw your mind out of the window but you do not have to try to understand everything.

Trust in the Lord with all your heart
And do not lean on your own understanding (Proverbs 3:5).

If I am honest, I leant to my own understanding virtually the whole of my life. I used my understanding to figure everything out, even my relationship with God. Eventually I gave up trying to understand: I just want to experience, and then everything I need to know will be revealed without me needing to try to find it for myself.

Four dimensions

There are four dimensions in which we will engage with the Father:

1. Engage in the earth, the physical realm, the here and now; but in the spiritual atmosphere of an open heaven.
2. Engage in our spirit and heart, the spiritual dimension. Our spirit and our soul is a realm in which God comes to dwell within us, a place where there is fellowship

21

and relationship, so we can engage God in us experientially.

3. Engage in the heavenly realms – in the Father's garden and any other places He may take us.
4. Engage God's heart in eternity, outside of time and space. This is where we were first thought of, as a desire in His heart and a thought in His mind. We were created there, so it feels like this is where we were always meant to be, where our origin is, and we can reconnect to it.

When we engage the Father in four different dimensions, it creates a window through which eternity (what was before there was) can manifest here and now to create what will be; so the end and beginning will be in agreement and history will unfold in alignment with the heart of the Father.

Engage in the earth

Let's practise the first of those now with an activation based on a story Jesus told. We can all encounter the loving Father just as the prodigal son did. This story is so much an expression of what the Father's heart really is, how He wants us to know we are accepted and to give us a ring of sonship. You may have come across this activation before, and you may even have experienced this many times, but it is an opportunity to be refreshed and be blessed.

We call these practice exercises 'activations' because they activate our imagination, which is the 'screen' on which we 'see' what is happening in the spirit. In all activations, we have found the best way is to find a comfortable position, relax, breathe deeply, loose our body from tension and loose our mind from over-analysing. No need to be concerned, this is not eastern meditation. Eastern meditation techniques often involve emptying your mind and allowing something to come and fill it. Christian meditation is totally the opposite: we fill our mind by fixing our thoughts on what we are looking to engage in. So focus your conscious thoughts on what you are seeking to engage, but do not strive to 'see' visually; just go with what forms in your imagination when it is focused on the Father (or on Jesus or on the Holy Spirit).

You may be aware of having thoughts, of seeing, hearing, feeling, sensing or knowing cognitively – or not – but your spirit will always receive more than you are consciously aware of. It is almost like a spiritual digestive system: our spirits process revelation at different rates, but at some future time we will eventually discover that we know something without being aware of when we acquired that knowledge: our spirit has digested what it received by revelation and has communicated it to our consciousness.

Activation #1: Prodigal son and loving Father

So he got up and came to his father. But while he was still a long way off, his father saw him and felt compassion for him, and ran and embraced him and kissed him (Luke 15:20).

When we do activations in a 'live' setting, we often play instrumental music in the background[1], as you will hear in the audio versions on the resources page. Close your eyes (read through the text first, or scan the QR code to listen to the audio version).

Relax and focus on the Father,
who has been waiting for you to come to Him.

Think of your loving heavenly Father running towards you, welcoming you with open arms to embrace and kiss you.

---

[1] We have included a link to suitable music tracks, composed and recorded for this purpose by Samuel Lane of SML Music (together with some other suggestions) on the resources page: freedomarc.org/etf-resources

That is what God longs to do with you!
Let that image form in your imagination.

But there may be some obstacles in the way,
issues that come between you
and prevent you engaging the Father in that way.
Allow any obstacles, any negative thoughts or negative
emotions, to come to your mind.

Take any sin, guilt, shame, condemnation,
disappointment, inadequacy, worry, anxiety, fear,
disapproval, or whatever you are feeling;
put them in a bag and hand them all over to Him.

Let Him embrace you in His arms of love.
Let Him speak words of life over you;
words of forgiveness and blessing.
Feel His love penetrate deeply into your heart.

Let Him clothe you with His love.
Let Him put a ring of sonship on your finger.
Feel the joy and pleasure of His heart for you.
Let Him release His love, joy and peace to you.

Let Him draw you deeper into His heart.
Let Him reveal more of His love for you.

Stay there as long as you want. If you fall asleep in any of these
engagements, do not worry! The best place to be is in a place
of rest, and sometimes when we drift into that edge-of-sleep
condition, that is when our spirit becomes more open.

Continually affirmed

As we engage the Father in this earthly, spiritual dimension,
we can be continually affirmed as sons of God living under an
open heaven, just as Jesus was affirmed by His Father.

*And behold, a voice out of the heavens said, "This is my beloved
Son in whom I am well pleased"* (Matthew 3:17).

Now God wants to say the same to each of us. Each of us is His beloved child, His beloved son or daughter, so each of us can receive that outworking of the desire and pleasure of His heart to affirm us and call us into our sonship. We are under an open heaven now and we can all receive the Father's affirmation. So when you hear those words, "You are My beloved son, and in you I am well pleased," receive them; do not fight against them, or think "But I'm not good enough." You are good enough because He has made you righteous. We do not have to be good enough in our own strength – that is impossible – but He has made us good enough to come into His presence.

Another version of that verse says "You bring me great joy" and yet another says "It is you in whom my soul delights." Receive that: His soul delights in you. That is how God is feeling about you right now. That is how He always feels about you. You may not feel that yourself, but take a few moments and let Him reveal that to you now.

"You are My son; in you I am well pleased."
"You who bring Me great joy."
"You in whom My soul delights."
"I take great delight in you."
"In you is My delight."

Progressive encounters

The encounters Jesus had with His Father in this realm were progressive. Matthew recounts another experience Jesus had under an open heaven when His Father again spoke to Him:

And He was transfigured before them; and His face shone like the sun, and His garments became as white as light. And behold, Moses and Elijah appeared to them, talking with Him... While he was still speaking, a bright cloud overshadowed them, and behold, a voice out of the cloud said, "This is My beloved Son, with whom I am well-pleased; listen to Him!" (Matthew 17:2-3, 5).

25

So it does not just have to be one experience of engaging the Father, it can be progressive; until you begin to shine, you begin to radiate the light, you begin to be transfigured. This was not just Jesus doing a 'Jesus thing', this was Jesus demonstrating what sonship is: being transfigured to radiate the light of God. Some people today are beginning to shine, they are being caught on camera radiating light, because their spirit is beginning to release that light from within them.

Let us not limit the possibilities of what can happen when we engage with the Father: as we continue to do so He is transfiguring us (the Greek word translated 'transfigured' here is *metamorphoo*, related to the word 'metamorphosis'), He is changing each of us from one degree of glory to another: from human beings into living beings, into spirit beings, into godlike beings. Through these encounters we can reconnect to God's original intent and purpose for us and for all creation. The more we engage with the Father, the more we will grow, just as Jesus Himself did.

The Child continued to grow and become strong, increasing in wisdom; and the grace of God was upon Him (Luke 2:40).

God wants to put His wisdom and grace upon us and He wants to overshadow us. Jesus started to discover this: when He went missing at the age of 12 and was found in the Temple, His response to His parents was quite interesting.

And He said to them, "Why did you seek Me? Did you not know that I must be about My Father's business?" (Luke 2:49 NKJV).

And Jesus kept increasing in wisdom and stature, and in favor with God and men (Luke 2:52).

The more we engage with God (even in this earthly realm), the more we will grow, the more we will mature, and the more we will begin to understand the nature of God and ourselves.

A convergence of time and eternity

God speaks from where He is to where we are, from where He is in eternity. He speaks to us through an open heaven, to reveal the truth from His perspective. It is His perspective and not ours, which is why it is important not to try to figure it out or try to understand it, but to receive it.

"But the Helper, the Holy Spirit, whom the Father will send in My name, He will teach you all things, and bring to your remembrance all that I said to you" (John 14:26).

Now you could assume that this only applies to the things that Jesus said to his disciples while He was on earth, or you can apply it to everything He has ever spoken to you about from all time in eternity. What He has spoken, even if you have never heard it, He can still bring it to your remembrance. Remember, He is speaking out of the 'eternal now,' but He is speaking into time so that you can engage with it.

There is a convergence of a time and eternity in the moment that He speaks; and He may speak words that you understand or He may just speak to your spirit, so that your spirit will be reignited with what it already knew but had forgotten. In either case, be open to receive it.

The Spirit of truth

"When the Helper comes, whom I will send to you from the Father, that is the Spirit of truth who proceeds from the Father, He will testify about Me, and you will testify also, because you have been with Me from the beginning" (John 15:26-27).

Again, you could assume this only applies to those particular disciples, or you could think no, we too have been with Him who was in the beginning with God, who was face to face with God in the beginning. Because the Word was with God in the beginning; therefore we too have been with Him from the beginning, so let's reconnect to that eternal relationship.

"But when He, the Spirit of truth, comes, He will guide you into all the truth... He will glorify Me, for He will take of Mine and will disclose it to you. All things that the Father has are Mine; therefore I said that He takes of Mine and will disclose it to you" (John 16:13-15).

He will reveal everything we need to know, whether it be cognitive or inspirational and creational in us, for each one of us to be able to fulfil our destiny and to know who we are as sons of God.

"'And it shall be in the last days,' God says, 'That I will pour forth of My Spirit on all mankind; and your sons and your daughters shall prophesy, and your young men shall see visions, and your old men shall dream dreams'" (Acts 2:17).

This time the scripture categorically says who this applies to, and it is 'all mankind,' not just believers. The Spirit of God is working in everybody to reveal Jesus who is at work in them, most people just do not know it yet. And we have not done such a good job of explaining it to them because we have been focused on telling them what they have done wrong, rather than revealing who they are as children of God. So we all, believers and unbelievers, are able to have remembrance of the things God has said, His thoughts about us revealed to us.

Activation #2: Under an open heaven

As we sit under an open heaven, God wants to speak to us His affirmation, acceptance, approval, recognition, commendation, recommendation, blessing, endorsement. He wants to speak out His validation of our sonship – not of all the things we might have done but of who we really are, because who we really are is nothing to do with what we might have done. God knows who we all are and He wants *you* to know who *you* are, separated from the works that you have done in this world, to take you back to the essence of that truth.

So sit under that open heaven and allow the Father to speak. A cloud of His presence is going to surround you: you are going to be enveloped in that cloud of His presence, that cloud of His glory. In that cloud, He is going to speak to you; to whisper things to you; to impart something to you: He is going to call forth your sonship.

Again, either scan the QR code, use the audio on the resources page, or read the following declarations and then spend some time (with your eyes closed if possible) receiving them into your spirit.

Begin to think of that open heaven.
Let that cloud of glory come around you,
let the Father's presence come around you
and receive these living words into your spirit:

"Son, I call your spirit to attention.
Spirit, listen as a true son.

"I call forth your identity as a son, part of the Joshua generation, the order of Melchizedek.

"I call forth your destiny to manifest God's kingdom on earth as it is in heaven.

"I call forth your destiny to fill the earth with God's glory.

"I call forth your identity, destiny and authority as lords to administer God's rule on earth as it is in heaven.

"I call forth your identity, destiny and authority as kings to have charge over God's heavenly courts.

"I call forth your identity, destiny and authority as sons to stand in My presence and be displayed on the earth.

"I call forth your identity, destiny and authority as sons of God to answer the groan of creation and restore it to original condition and purpose.

29

"I call forth the Joshua Generation to rise up and take possession of their inheritance.

"You are My beloved son in whom My soul delights and I am well pleased with you.

"Receive My acceptance, affirmation, approval, recognition, recommendation, commendation, blessing, endorsement and validation.

"I speak words of remembrance from My eternal heart to you."

In this chapter we have begun to engage with God in the earth realm, under an open heaven. Do continue to practise this and make it part of your daily lifestyle. But we will now go on to also engage Him in the dimensions within us, in our spirit and in our heart.

3. Engage in Dimensions Within

For when He received honor and glory from God the Father, such an utterance as this was made to Him by the Majestic Glory, "This is My beloved Son with whom I am well-pleased" - and we ourselves heard this utterance made from heaven when we were with Him on the holy mountain.

So we have the prophetic word made more sure, to which you do well to pay attention as to a lamp shining in a dark place, until the day dawns and the morning star arises in your hearts (2 Peter 1:17-19).

This is a transition from engaging God here in the earth realm to engaging God within our hearts and knowing Him there. Wherever we are, we can have the same intimacy that we just experienced in the previous activations; and we can have that intimacy within, all the time, because He is in us. He wants us to live in that intimate relationship continually, so that we are never alone, we never have to be fearful, we never have to feel in any way separated from Him because He has chosen to come and dwell in us.

"In that day you will know that I am in My Father, and you in Me, and I in you..." Jesus answered and said to him, "If anyone loves Me, he will keep My word; and My Father will love him, and We will come to him and make Our abode with him" (John 14:20, 23).

The Father, Son and Spirit have come to dwell in our spirit, which (like Dr Who's Tardis) is bigger on the inside than on the outside. We may have a physical body within which our soul and spirit are contained, but in reality our spirit is a much bigger dimensional place.

You may have heard me speak about having a garden in your heart, which can be many acres of cultivated space. Or, if you have never cultivated anything within the garden of your heart, it might be a little patch of weeds, with a few stones and hard areas thrown in! In the parable of the sower, Jesus talked

31

about the soil of our heart having four conditions: hard, stony, weedy and good; so there may be some areas of our heart which are cultivated and really beautiful places and others which are not quite as pleasing. As a house of God and a gateway of heaven, God dwells within us and He wants us to cultivate the ground so that all our heart is good.

First love

We need to cultivate this first love relationship.

"To the angel of the church in Ephesus write... 'you have perseverance and have endured for My name's sake, and have not grown weary. But I have this against you, that you have left your first love'" (Revelation 2:1a, 3-4).

Here in Revelation, Jesus' message to the Ephesian church acknowledged all the amazing things they were doing and yet, He said, they had left their first love. Now, if any of you can remember first love in a natural sense and what it felt like, and then multiply it a few billion times, that is what God wants you to feel in His first love. In experiencing how He loves you, you can actually love Him back and fully express your love to Him without any restrictions or limitations, without the hindrances of hurt and damage which many of us have because of our broken relationships and broken hearts. God wants to restore our hearts so that we can receive His love and express our love for Him unrestricted by any brokenness.

We also have another scripture in Revelation:

"Behold, I stand at the door and knock; if anyone hears My voice and opens the door, I will come in to him and will dine with him, and he with Me. He who overcomes, I will grant to him to sit down with Me on My throne, as I also overcame and sat down with My Father on His throne" (Revelation 3:20-21).

That is the invitation to open the door in our spirit to allow the presence of God to fill us, Father, Son and Spirit. And then, when our spirit is full, it can flow through our soul, filling the garden of our heart and all the other aspects of our soul with His presence. Then as we enter into relationship and get to know God in that first love intimacy, He will lead us into a place where we are seated in the realms of heaven in authority, in our kingdom governmental position there.

Garden of our heart

So we can invite the Father to engage our soul within the garden of our heart. If you don't know where it is, He will tell you – in fact He will show you and take you there if you ask.

When I first spent time in the garden of my heart I had no idea where I was. I thought I was in some special little place in heaven that God had made just for me and Him, with a tree swing and a little bench and a small patch of grass. I would sit on the swing and He would push me and talk with me and tell me things. It was amazing because I never had that in my natural childhood so He knew exactly what I needed, to have a special place with my Dad. Then one day He asked "Do you know where we are?" I guessed that we were somewhere in heaven, but He said, "No, we're in the garden of your heart."

The garden of my heart? I did not even know I had one – but then I realised why it was such a small place! Now the garden of my heart is cultivated and full of things I have planted there, things I have created there. Everything I do in heaven is reflected in the garden of my heart: there are even mountains in my garden. It is a reflection of heaven, just as Adam's garden was supposed to be a reflection of Eden.

The River of Life was flowing out of Eden into Adam's garden. The River of Life flows out of heaven into our spirit, but because most of us have never learned to open that first love gate it has been like a trickle under the threshold. Most of us have lived off that trickle: all the gifts of the Spirit and the fruit of the Spirit we have experienced have come through that trickle. But in Ezekiel 47 we see that God desires it to be ankle deep, knee deep, waist deep, a river no one could cross – flowing and bringing life wherever it goes. So far most of us do not have rivers of living water flowing out of our innermost

33

being, we have a trickle. That trickle is amazing, but what would it be like if it were a flood?

That is why it is good to learn to open that door, that first love gate, on a daily basis and invite His presence to fill us and flow through us. It will create an atmosphere of love so that when people come near us they will sense God's presence, His love, joy and peace, emanating from us.

Cultivate and tend

Just as Adam had a garden to cultivate and tend, so too do we. We are supposed to tend the garden of our heart, to look after it and make sure that the ground in there is good soil. And if there are hard areas which have been trodden down and damaged because of broken hearts, broken trust and all the things that happen to us in this life, then sometimes it is really hard for God to plant all the things that He wants for us, or for us to plant them. There may be memories stored in our heart which are negative and which hinder the development of the real fruit and truth.

If you invite Him to, and if you cooperate with Him, God will take you on a journey in which He will deal with the soil of your heart so that it is all good ground. Then everything you encounter in God can become planted in your heart and produce fruit that you can eat and give away to others, which is what testimony is all about.

Walking in the garden

They heard the sound of the Lord God walking in the garden in the cool of the day... (Genesis 3:8a).

I believe that Adam and Eve heard that sound every day of their existence, right up until the day mentioned in this passage, when they felt the need to go and hide in the bushes and cover up. Even at that point, God did not say to them, "What have you done?" but "Where are you?" and if they had responded, "Here we are," and come back to Him, He would have restored them and made them totally whole. They did

34

not do that, they continued to try to cover up – and humanity has been trying to do the same ever since. But we have an opportunity of walking again in the garden with our Father in the cool of the day, a time of refreshing in which we engage with Him.

Indeed, the Lord will comfort Zion;
He will comfort all her waste places.
And her wilderness He will make like Eden,
And her desert like the garden of the Lord;
Joy and gladness will be found in her,
Thanksgiving and sound of a melody (Isaiah 51:3).

... And you will be like a watered garden,
And like a spring of water whose waters do not fail
(Isaiah 58:11b).

That is what He wants the garden of your heart to be like and if you let Him, He will help you to get there. And that is also what the world is looking for: people who have wonderful springs of life and salvation flowing out and filling the world.

Psalm 23

When you lie down in your garden, Psalm 23 is a really good place to start.

The Lord is my shepherd,
I shall not want.
He makes me lie down in green pastures;
He leads me beside quiet waters.
He restores my soul;
He guides me in the paths of righteousness
For His name's sake (Psalm 23:1-3).

"He makes me lie down in green pastures"– it is not a suggestion. We really do need to learn to rest, so sometimes He will sit on us or pin us down to stop us moving because we are just overactive all the time. He would much rather we do it voluntarily, that we would have a desire and make a choice to find an oasis of rest every day and live from that place.

The quiet waters, that is the River of Life; and if we open up our first love gate it will not just be a trickle in our garden but a river that we can drink from and bathe in. As we will see (and experience) later, we can actually follow it all the way back to its source and go back into Eden.

He restores our soul. He guides us, because He wants us to be a true reflection and representation of Himself and bring glory and honour to His name.

Activation #3: Open the door

To listen to the audio version, scan the QR code (right) with your phone camera, or use the link from the resources page. Or simply read through the text of the activation below before closing your eyes.

Behold, I stand at the door and knock; if anyone hears My voice and opens the door, I will come in to him and will dine with him, and he with Me (Revelation 3:20).

Close your eyes and think of that door in your spirit.
Let that door form in your imagination.
The handle of the door is on your side.
By faith reach out to the handle and choose to open the first love gate.

As you open the door,
that river of living water begins to flow.
Welcome the Father's presence into your spirit.
Allow your whole being, spirit, soul and body,
to engage Him in a loving embrace.

Invite the Father to take you into the garden of your heart.
Let Him lead you to the green pastures
or to your secret place.

As you lie down and rest,
resting in the Father's presence in your garden,
let Him begin to restore your soul
to face-to-face blameless innocence,
revealing wonderful truths to you of who you are.

Every night I send my soul into the garden of my heart to lie down with my Shepherd in green pastures. My spirit is active in heaven, and I go to sleep. When I awake, sometimes I am aware of the conversations we have had during the night, and sometimes not. But I have set my soul in a place where it can engage with God all night; you can do the same. I encourage you to try it for yourself tonight.

4. Engage in Heavenly Realms

We have engaged with the physical realm and the dimensions within, so now we are going into the spiritual realm. The spiritual realm interacts with the physical realm, but it is not limited to a particular space or time.

There are many things which you cannot see with your physical eyes but which you can with the eyes of your heart or the eyes of your spirit. When I am in a roomful of people, I can see everyone there with my natural eyes, but I can also see things around them with my spiritual eyes. I can see the colours and the angels, and if I choose to, I can see what everyone is carrying or manifesting in the spirit.

Come up here

We can engage the Father in the heavenly dimensions because the veil is torn. Jesus tore the veil between heaven and earth and it says in John 10 that He is the door and we are to go in and out of that door to find pasture. So we can go in and out of the realms of heaven, the spiritual realms, because He has made them available to us and invited us to come.

After these things I looked, and behold, a door standing open in heaven, and the first voice which I had heard, like the sound of a trumpet speaking with me, said, "Come up here, and I will show you what must take place after these things" (Revelation 4:1).

His invitation to John was to "Come up here." God does not treat us any differently or show favouritism, so we all have that same invitation. You can see this again in Hebrews:

Therefore let us draw near with confidence to the throne of grace, so that we may receive mercy and find grace to help in time of need (Hebrews 4:16).

I know we traditionally use that verse to refer to prayer. Most of our 'coming boldly' has involved calling out to God and asking Him from this earthly realm, hoping that He hears. But

38

the writer to the Hebrews is not speaking theoretically. The Throne of Grace is a real throne in the heavenly realms: we can go there, actually sit on the Father's lap and sense His presence. So many people pray and are not really sure whether their prayers are going beyond the ceiling. When you are talking to God face-to-face it is very different; and He wants us all to experience Him like that.

He has opened up that realm for us and we do not have to physically die before we go there. Spiritually we have become alive, we have been resurrected; and that resurrection life in Christ has given us access to that realm. We can engage in the Garden of Eden, in the waterfalls, in the River of Life, at the Tree of Life, the Throne of Grace, the Judgment Seat... there are so many different places which are now so much a part of me that I can just access them.

But when I was learning these things, I walked along paths with Jesus and He took me where He wanted me to go. Heaven is such an amazing place. It is full of fragrance and life beyond the colours and fragrances of this realm. Everything is living and active, so you walk along the path and the path is alive and the path is blessing you!

Am I just imagining this?

You may be wondering, am I sure I am not just imagining this? Using our imagination as a screen for an experience to outwork is different from trying to imagine something. We can all use our imagination to imagine something, but when we do activations and engagements we use our imagination to picture something which then becomes a doorway we can step through. And when we do step through, we are not trying to make anything up, we are actually experiencing it.

Have you ever had a prophetic picture in your mind? If so, where did that come from? Did you imagine it or was it projected into your mind by the Spirit? The Spirit projected it there so that you could see it. Visions are a projection onto the screen of your imagination too, a projection of something that God wants you to see. So at the beginning of the book of Revelation, John was looking into heaven as a vision and seeing amazing things but then he had the invitation to "come up here." That is when he stepped through what he was seeing, right into the spirit realm, which is different from seeing the spirit realm as a vision.

Because of practice

You have to practise these things.

But solid food is for the mature, who because of practice have their senses trained to discern good and evil (Hebrews 5:14).

Our whole *Engaging God*[2] programme is about practising to get your spiritual senses working. But when you step through, what you get is what you get. Sometimes that can be very visual, and at other times you do not necessarily see visually but you are sensing something, you are feeling something: you are there, you are engaging, but you are not necessarily seeing it in what you might think of as a vision. You may not perhaps see it as a full-blown Hollywood movie production, because sometimes it does not come that way but as a more subtle perception of what is there and what is going on.

When I say "what you get is what you get," the key is to just receive whatever it is and however it comes. Receive, do not try to analyse it, and do not reject it because you think you should be getting something different or because you are not seeing how or what you think someone else is seeing. Just rest in it.

Of course, sometimes encounters happen involuntarily, especially in the beginning. When I first went into heaven I fell into a trance just sitting at my desk in the office. I was totally unaware of my surroundings and I was in heaven. I

---

[2] Find out more at eg.freedomarc.org/freetrial

could have been in heaven bodily for all I knew! I could not make a trance happen. I was seeking God for intimacy with Him and He helped by doing that for me.

I would not encourage you to seek for trances or try to make them happen by some technical formula. If you fall into a trance because God wants to suspend the present reality to take you into another one and He does that, great. But we cannot be dependent on trances to live our lives: we want to be living in the realms of heaven by choice.

So for me it has gone beyond involuntary encounters to learning how to do that for myself. "Heaven is open, I have an invitation so I am going to come." I step out in faith on that invitation, enter into that heavenly realm, and whatever I experience, I experience. Then I can share some of my experiences, which hopefully encourage you to engage these things for yourself.

You really do need to experience them yourself, so whatever Jesus wants to do with you when you ask Him to take you somewhere, go with it and don't overthink it or try to make it happen, just be in faith that something is happening. The more experienced you are, and the more practice you have put in, and the more able your spiritual eyes are to see and your spiritual ears to hear, the easier it gets.

After that first experience in a trance in 2008 I did not have another encounter for two years. Over those next two years I desperately tried to get back there: I did not know how, but I pursued it and I set the desire of my heart on it. Eventually God took me back there and showed me how I could do it whenever I wanted.

It is open for all of us, but it is not magic and it does not just materialise: you have to train your senses and it takes time to do that. So for now you will be able to engage these things at whatever level you are. Just go with that; as you keep practising you will find you engage more and more.

41

The angelic

Are they not all ministering spirits, sent out to render service for the sake of those who will inherit salvation? (Hebrews 1:14)

Let us look now at how we engage and interact with the angelic realm. As we read in that verse, God has given us the angels to be ministering spirits on our behalf, and if we do not learn how to engage them we will not enjoy the full benefit of their help. They will always be helping behind the scenes, but they want to be much more actively involved with us.

And He said to him, "Truly, truly, I say to you, you will see the heavens opened and the angels of God ascending and descending on the Son of Man" (John 1:51).

Jesus lived under an open heaven and interacted with the angels throughout His earthly life. We too have an open heaven for a manifestation of God's glory (which goes beyond His presence) and we want to invite Him to be here.

We welcome the Father, the Son and the Holy Spirit to be with us.

We also welcome the seven spirits of God:

- The Spirit of the Lord
- The Spirit of Wisdom
- The Spirit of Understanding
- The Spirit of Counsel
- The Spirit of Might
- The Spirit of Knowledge
- The Spirit of the Fear of the Lord.

These are seven created beings, tutors and trainers who will help us engage with our sonship and bring us into maturity.

We welcome any of the cloud of witnesses who would like to participate with us.

We welcome the four angels, or orders of angels, who have been assigned to this season to help us transition:

- Transformation
- Winds of Change
- Sound of Many Waters
- Refiner's Fire.

We welcome the four living creatures, a representation of the four faces of God:

- Lion (king)
- Ox (oracle)
- Eagle (legislator)
- Man (priest)

These represent God's government, the kingly, the priestly, the oracle and the legislative government of God. We welcome their presence, because if they can help then we need all the help we can get! But we need also to learn to engage, and to experience how to engage with them.

Activation #4: The angelic (unguided)

When we did this exercise at the first *Sons Arise!* conference, we set flags and banners out on the floor to represent them. You may not have flags and banners, but as you look at the following diagrams, engage wherever your spirit is drawn.

Again, do not try to understand, but allow your spirit to guide you. You are stepping into the heavenly realm and you will experience that interaction in a way which is personal for you.

There is no format to what will happen or how. Just focus on (for example) the lion, saying in your mind, "I want to engage with the lion" and then allow whatever happens to happen.

You will find colour versions of these images and a range of suggested suitable instrumental music to accompany your engagements on the resources page (which you can access online at freedomarc.org/etf-resources).

43

Winds of Change

Transformation

Sound of many waters

Refiners Fire

The central flag above features swirling colours of the rainbow.

Seven Spirits of God

Spirit of Wisdom

Spirit of Counsel

Prepares us for position

Spirit of Might

Authorises us for position

Reveals us for position

Spirit of Wisdom

Spirit of Knowledge

Equips us for position

Empowers us for position

Spirit of the Fear of the Lord

Spirit of the Lord

Mandates us for position

Brings us into accountability for position

These flags are coloured (from left to right)
red, orange, yellow, green, blue, indigo and violet.

Do not try to predetermine what your experience will be, and if it does not happen the way you expect, do not be concerned. You may experience some very specific thoughts or feelings in your body or not consciously feel anything. Engage by faith, because God always responds and rewards our faith, so you will receive something even if you are not aware of it. Take a few minutes now to engage.

I encourage you to come back to this exercise as often as you wish, and engage with something different each time, so that you become familiar with how it feels to interact with different angelic beings in different places and dimensions.

More heavenly places

Within Eden there is the Father's garden, a 'garden within the garden,' and we can go there. It is the most beautiful place of rest, peace and intimacy in which He connects with His creation.

There are the fire stones mentioned in Ezekiel 28, which we will engage with in chapter 10.

We can go into the throne room of Revelation 4:5 where the four living creatures are; the seven spirits of God, the thunders and lightnings and the sea of glass. When I go there I am on my face casting my crowns before the awesomeness of God as King and Creator.

We can engage the Holy of Holies. We can step in there and engage the Arc of the presence of God, the cherubim forming an arc, opening a portal for God's presence. There we can encounter the four faces of God: Lion, Ox, Eagle and Man, and the *Yod Hei Vav Hei* of God's name in which we can stand and engage governmentally.

We tend to teach these things in an order of progression, which is not always how you experience them. God just took me to places: I did not know where they were and to get back there I had to continue to re-engage and practise, practise,

45

practise. That had to become my lifestyle, but once I learned how to do it then I could do it all the time.

We can engage the Father in the various courts of heaven because we are called to have charge of the courts. Heaven operates, like most governmental systems, with courts and councils. There are many different courts, and in chapter 14 we will engage with the Court of the Lord, the *Sod*[3] of God. That is probably the highest court you can engage in, although we are not going there legislatively, just experientially to connect with our destiny scroll. That is where we were assigned our scroll and agreed it before we came into this physical realm; it is where our angels were assigned to us, and it is good to reconnect with that destiny now.

We can re-engage with our scroll there and discover the timeline of our life. We can then access the Father on the ancient paths, on the Way of Life, walking back through the eternal circle of what was into what is and into what will be to access the heart of God.

I have seen the task which God has given the sons of men with which to occupy themselves. He has made everything appropriate in its time. He has also set eternity in their heart... (Ecclesiastes 3:10-11a)

So all of us have been given a destiny which we are to outwork appropriately in its time, and He has placed within us access to eternity and the desire to re-engage with where we came from. That is what everyone wants to hear: who am I, where did I come from, and why am I here? Those are the questions people ask all the time. God wants us to really know who He made us to be.

We can go back into the eternal heart and mind of God, where His desire birthed us each uniquely and individually in that

---

[3] *Sod* The Hebrew word *Sod* has a long 'o' as in 'code'.

place of His desire, where His thoughts about us formed us and He called us into being. We can re-engage with that. And we can listen to the conversation that Father, Son and Spirit are having about us now. We may not necessarily pick up everything they say but we can get little snippets of things that we need to hear because they connect us to where we are in our journey.

The relationship between Father, Son and Spirit is sometimes described as 'the circle of the dance.' It is active, living, vibrant and full of the joy of life. We can participate in it because we are invited back into the relationship we had there with Them in the beginning, to re-engage with it and begin to discern all the vast sum of God's thoughts towards us.

How precious also are Your thoughts to me, O God!
How vast is the sum of them! (Psalm 139:17).

I love that psalm because it describes how we are connected to God, how He thinks about us and how He sees us. He wants us to reconnect so that we see ourselves from His perspective and then also live from His perspective.

Covenant

This eternity symbol or lemniscate is a symbol of covenant. In the Old Testament when they made covenants they would walk through this figure of eight. You can see this when God came, put Abraham into a deep sleep and made a covenant with him, then walked with a fiery torch through the shed blood of the sacrifice which confirmed the covenant. Now we are in the New Covenant: Jesus has shed His blood and His blood on the Mercy Seat is a testimony in heaven of our salvation and our access to Him in relationship; that we can stand in Him.

So we can stand in what is (and 'what is' is not what is here on earth, but what is in heaven); then as we go back from 'what is' into 'what was' was, we can discover what God's desire and heart is for us every day from an eternal perspective, unbounded by everything we are seeing in this earthly realm. This is normally not cognitive for me, I am just there within that amazing relationship of love and conversation which informs who I am. Then I can take that back into the 'what is'; and, standing in the name of God, in the four faces, I can start to legislate. I can start to call my life into agreement with the heart of God and I can begin to shape things around me to create my reality. In that way, 'what will be' should be a representation of 'what was' was; but for it to be so we have to bring it into heaven and administrate it and call it into being so that then we can walk it out.

That is not something I am expecting everyone to understand, or to know how to do if you have never done it before, but this is where we are heading in this book (and series of books). God wants you to know and express His heart as a son and then to live out and walk out His heart, to create life. We should be history makers, so that history can be aligned with God's desire and not with the chaos that has been made by humanity walking in independence.

Enemies in the mind

So the question is, do we believe the vast sum of God's thoughts towards us? Do we really believe what He thinks about us as sons or are we believing the lies of an orphan spirit? We were all born thinking we were separated from God and that is what religion has emphasised: whatever religion you may be part of, including the religion we know as

'Evangelical Christianity', you will have had to go on some sort of works-based mission to get back to God and be reconnected to Him. The reality is that He has never been separated from us: we are only separated from Him because we think we are.

*And you once being **alienated and enemies in the mind** in the evil works yet now He reconciled* (Colossians 2:21. Literal translation without the usual added punctuation, emphasis mine).

For as he thinks in his heart, so is he (Proverbs 23:7a NKJV).

Do not be conformed to this world (this age), [fashioned after and adapted to its external, superficial customs], but be transformed (changed) by the [entire] renewal of your mind [by its new ideals and its new attitude], so that you may prove [for yourselves] what is the good and acceptable and perfect will of God, even the thing which is good and acceptable and perfect [in His sight for you] (Romans 12:2 AMPC).

God is with us and in us, and there is no need for separation. But we tend to believe the image we have about ourselves and into which the world (or properly, 'the age' – that is, the social, religious and political framework in which we live) has shaped and conformed us.

We need to be confident in our relationship with God that we can be everything He calls us to be and do everything He calls us to do. As we really connect with Him, He reveals what He thinks and believes about us. We need that transformation by the renewing of our minds so that we no longer believe what we have been conformed to but agree with and believe what God believes about us.

God believes in you more than you believe in yourself, and certainly more than anyone else believes in you. Our agreement and cooperation with His belief in us is where our sonship begins to become unveiled and to outwork.

5. Depth of the Father's Heart

No quick fix

In all we are doing, in every activation and in all the *Engaging God* program that we run, we are not offering you a shortcut or a quick fix of sonship. You cannot just get a dose of sonship and all of a sudden you know everything! It is a relationship. As we have seen, you can only be a son in relation to the reality that you have a Father and you are in relationship with Him. Your sonship has to be walked out in relationship. Reading this book can help you discover how to have that relationship but it is down to you to actually pursue it.

If we spend five minutes a week building our relationship with the Father, then our ability to know ourselves as sons is going to be five minutes a week's worth (which really is not that much). God wants to woo us and draw us in love to experience that relationship so that we want more and more – and then we can live in and from that relationship. It will not just be in our quiet time every morning (or our noisy time, depending on our inclination) but He wants us to walk with Him and live with Him all the time.

But the one who joins himself to the Lord is one spirit with Him (1 Corinthians 6:17).

So His intention is for our spirit to be one with Him. When we are joined to Him in fellowship, relationship and intimacy, we are connected to Him; we never need to be separated from Him at all. Of course, He is in us, so we are never separated in that way; but He wants us to enjoy a deeper relationship, so that we are continually flowing out of the relationship we have, and not continually trying to get one.

I have experienced these things as a forerunner and I want to make it easier for other people to have their own encounters. That is my mission in life, if you like: to try to open this up and make it accessible to you and many others as a doorway you can go through, to take up the opportunity to access these pathways for yourself, and to discover all the possibilities that exist there for you of deeper intimacy and relationship.

Eventually that will lead into responsibility but it is a process and a journey: you are not suddenly going to find yourself at the destination one day when it will all just happen. That was a charismatic illusion that was sold to us, that you can get someone to lay hands on you and you will 'get what they have'. Like many of us, I have been there, done that, got the hat, the T-shirt and the CD, and tried getting every man and his dog to lay hands on me. Yes, some of it was great but nothing ever lasted unless I pursued it for myself.

So all that I have done in recent years of my life, all that I have learned to hear and see and engage in heaven, I cannot impart it to you so that you will have what I have. What I can say is that it is possible for you to have everything that I have, and more besides, but you are going to have to develop it yourself and it takes time to do that development.

If I share how to hear God's voice, I can do it in two or three sentences, as my testimony, but in real time it took me five or six years to actually hear His voice. I am a tenacious person who does not easily give up, so if I do not do it the first time then I will go and go again until I do. When God started to speak to me and tried to get me to learn how to engage Him personally through speaking to Him, the only way I could do that was through the Bible. That was the only route I had, so I meditated on the Bible and God spoke to me through it, not just in a disconnected way but in a very personal way: His words, His thoughts, would form in my mind when I started to meditate on a passage. He spoke to me in a different way than when I was preparing a sermon or studying a scripture: these were His words in my mind, in a conversation.

Eventually I went beyond always needing to go through the Bible to talk to God into just talking to Him but it did not happen overnight. For a long time I never even thought about talking to Him as if He was in front of me: it just did not enter my mind. He talked to me through the Bible, He talked to me

51

through prophetic words and pictures and so on, but it was not like He was sitting there with me.

Having learned to hear His thoughts in scripture, one day I decided that I was going to put a chair opposite me and just accept that Jesus was there. I was not imagining Him there visually at this point in time, but I started to talk to Him as if He was there. I locked my office door because I did not want anyone to walk in on that process and think I was going a bit crazy, talking to an empty chair.

Nothing happened the first few times but I told myself that if I could hear God speak to me in the Bible, then I was sure I could hear Him speak to me without it. As I continued, I started asking Him questions, nothing deep or meaningful like the meaning of life, just very simple things. Then I started to get the same thoughts in conversation in my mind that I got when I was meditating in scripture. We started to have conversations, at which point it was better for me to stop asking and start listening, because He has an awful lot more to say than I have to ask.

So I just started to say, "Is there anything you want to talk to me about?" and we built up a relationship in which, as Jesus said, "My sheep can hear My voice." So now I could hear His voice and whilst I could ask Him things and hear Him reply, sometimes He would not give me the answer I wanted but would tell me something I needed to know.

Then eventually it opened up. It went beyond just an empty chair and believing that Jesus was there even though I could not see Him, into actually engaging visually.

Picture a beach

Again it was a process, and the way it began was completely unexpected. I went to a conference in London on the topic of social enterprise, how to set up social businesses to help people in their lives. I felt particularly drawn to the title of one seminar. It was being led by an Anglican vicar, but after he had introduced himself, he said, "We're not going to do the subject on the schedule, instead we're going to do a visual meditation to engage with God." And I thought "I didn't sign up for that! I didn't come all this way for you to do some stupid exercise!" I had a seriously bad attitude. So I was sitting there and God said to me, "And I asked him to do that just for you." So I said "I'm really sorry."

As soon as the speaker started the exercise, I could easily believe it had been designed just for me, because He said, "Close your eyes and picture a beach." I was brought up in a seaside town that had five beaches, and I had a favourite beach there, so it was really easy for me to picture that beach. "Walk on the beach, walk on the sand," and he described it very poetically. "And the wind is blowing..." and I realised, "Wow! I'm feeling this, I'm engaged in this!"

"Walk up to the water's edge. The water is lapping over your feet and someone is walking along the shore towards you. As they get closer to you, you see that it's Jesus..."

So I was seeing all this, and it was just like a picture in my mind which I engaged in. I pictured the beach and then I just followed along and there I was, walking on it. Eventually he said, "Jesus kneels down and draws or writes something in the sand." I looked, and what He wrote was "I love you." I saw that and I felt it, it really got into my heart.

After that experience, I wondered how I could do it again. I did that beach exercise a few times, but I could not seem to do anything else. So I thought I would try meditating in the Bible, finding scenes in scripture that I could picture and begin to engage. My meditations became visual, not just auditory, and then one day I was thinking about Jesus teaching His disciples and thought "Wouldn't it be wonderful to sit at the feet of Jesus and let Him teach me!"

So I found the passage I was thinking of, I started picturing it, and then Jesus looked at me. Right in my eyes. I suddenly realised, "He can see me! This is not just me picturing it, I'm interacting in it." Then He started to talk to me and teach me.

After that, whenever Jesus sat in the chair in my office, I could see Him and engage Him because it had moved on from "by faith I'm engaging and something's happening" to now "I'm engaging and this has gone beyond..."

This was all part of my journey. I am just sharing these things to encourage you that all of us can hear His voice, all of us can see what He is doing and He wants all of us to be engaged. Hearing my testimony can kick start this for you, but you are going to have to practise to develop your own experiences.

You have to find what works for you, because we are all wired differently. We can all talk to God at the same time, and He will interact with everyone personally and individually; and we can all join in an activation and each get something different because God will reveal what each one of us uniquely needs to receive, and He will do so in a way that we can personally receive it.

For such a time

I mentioned that we are going to engage with some of the cloud of witnesses. Esther turned up at a meeting of Freedom Church one Sunday morning; I became aware of her presence and I went to talk to her. Now you might think that is really weird, but we have read how Moses and Elijah appeared on a mountain top one day and Jesus had a conversation with them, and He said we would do the things that He did (and greater), so why not? As I was talking to Esther, what came to mind was this sentence from her life story:

"Yet who knows whether you have come to the kingdom for such a time as this?" (Esther 4:14b NKJV).

I asked her why she had come, and she said, "I wanted to remind everyone in the room that you're all called for a time such as this, that you all have a destiny."

Now I believe that the sons of God are called to mature and engage kingship for a time such as this, and I am sure that Esther is going to be taking a keen interest in who responds to this, so you may find that you can hang out with her and she will give you some insight into engaging with your destiny. If she shows up for you, or you sense something, just go with it and see what happens.

I was not content with just the few minutes of conversation I had with Esther that morning, so I went to seek her out in heaven. I found her in the Court of the Upright (where the men in white linen often gather as the cloud of witnesses) and this is what she told me:

"I was unprepared despite all the attention of the court. It was not until I was placed in the position to step out into my destiny in God that I truly discovered who I was within God's kingdom and what I was capable of."

In other words, she did not really know who she was until she was thrust into the situation. And sometimes God does that, He throws you in at the deep end and you have to sink or swim (sometimes He even lets you sink, to show you that you cannot do it in your own strength).

And she went on, "I didn't see the process as something to be desired, and the outcome wasn't what I was expecting. Many people fail to recognize their own destiny until they're in the midst of it."

She did not want to be the concubine or the wife of the king. Even when she was taken and put into that position, she still did not see where it was leading.

Following this second conversation with her, I went to talk to the Father and asked Him about it. He said, "Son, use the *Sons Arise!* environment to accelerate the process of my children being prepared for their sonship positions. Let me call people beyond their present expectations and take them out of the comfort of their boats into the uncharted water where they will learn to swim without aids. I will stretch my children beyond, if you will provide the environment where they are safe to explore."

You can choose to stay in the boat; you can choose to stay safe and secure while the storms rage around you. But He wants you to step out of the boat and walk on the water. Just as Esther went through a process of purification to prepare her, so Jesus has already made us righteous and worthy to access the King. We do not have to do anything. We do not have to make ourselves better. We just have to be, and allow Him to engage with us. Esther did not desire it yet she still entered into it, but God is giving us the opportunity to find and kindle that desire.

Do we want more of a deep relationship with our Father, the King? Do we believe we are worthy or do we believe the lies that tell us we are less than worthy? Sometimes that is what will stop us. We will not think that God wants to speak to us or bring us into that intimacy because of what other people have said, or what we think about ourselves. It is what God thinks about us that is important, so let's take the time to listen to Him and take notice of what He says. Let that change the way we think. Our thinking will never be changed by trying to do it ourselves. I used to try to change my mind by putting little scriptures up all over the place and reading and confessing them all the time. I learned to memorise a lot of Bible verses that way but it never changed my mind.

At that time my Bible was full of underlining and highlighting of passages which had really spoken to me. Eventually, God challenged me. "Why do you treat your Bible like a filing cabinet? Do you know any of those things by experience? I started to speak to you through them and you underlined them and you highlighted them and you preached on them but you never engaged them." That was when I started to learn to meditate, and everything took off from there. Encounters like this may be significant milestones on our journey, and we will all have our own; we will remember that God did this or such and such happened and that was what stirred us to go deeper and move forward.

Legislation for the Depth of the Father's Heart

Another piece of legislation I produced as God prepared me to bring this *Sons Arise!* message was legislation for the depths of the Father's heart. He has been drawing me into His heart, wooing me into an intimacy with Him for a long time, so this is really nothing new. I was living in Cornwall when God broke in with us, the year before it happened in Toronto, and it was weird, wild, wacky stuff. We did a lot of laughing, a lot of crying, a lot of being stuck to the floor and so on, but in it all God was trying to get our attention, to call us back into intimacy, to discover the intimacy of sonship and discover His Fatherhood. We enjoyed the experiences but got so caught up on the manifestations that we did not really get the point of it. Still, that was all part of my journey as well.

Here is that legislation:

You are authorised to release a new wave of intimacy.

You are authorised to call for deep calls to deep.

You are authorised to rip open the hearts of men with the power of love.

You are authorised to call orphans to come home into the adoption of sonship.

You are authorised to call for the removal of masks that hide the orphan spirit.

You are authorised to call for open heart surgery to remove the hardness of damaged hearts.

You are authorised to undo the yokes and remove the heavy burdens of the slavery mentality.

You are authorised to release the love of the Father to broken hearts.

You are authorised to pour out the balm of the Father's heart to heal brokenness.

You are authorised to administrate the eternal love of God to call My children back to their eternal identity as sons of light.

For a while I had been producing legislation for one person or another, or for a particular group, but I knew this was especially for me. Of course, it was for others as well, but when I started decreeing it I began to experience a new wave of intimacy myself.

This law authorises me to release all this and also authorises other people to take it and use it themselves. There are areas of jurisdiction for the laws that we have, but most of the ones I get are for the Joshua generation, so if you are being called to cross over into the realm of heaven and experience the reality of sonship – which, if you have read this far, you probably recognise that you are – then this is authorisation for you to receive and release this law too.

I need the balm of the Father's heart to heal brokenness in me. I need the fragmented parts of me to be integrated and made whole. Everything I bring always starts with me, and everything must always start with you too. Then we have a testimony and authority to release it. This is why it cannot be theoretical: you do not have any authority in theory, it has to be outworked in practice and then that can be administrated.

Are you willing?

This is what God asked me, so I will ask you:

Are you willing to get on the altar and ask God to do an open-heart surgery on you?

Are you willing to let the love of God be like healing balm administered to any brokenness in your heart?

You may have gone through years of inner healing and forgiveness ministry, as I did for many years, but until I met God face to face He never got to the depth He has now.

So where is this altar? There many altars in the realms of heaven. There is an altar in the tabernacle of heaven which represents the cross. But there is also an altar in the temple that Isaiah went to in this familiar scripture:

In the year of King Uzziah's death I saw the Lord sitting on a throne, lofty and exalted, with the train of His robe filling the temple. Seraphim stood above Him, each having six wings: with two he covered his face, and with two he covered his feet, and with two he flew. And one called out to another and said,

"Holy, Holy, Holy, is the Lord of hosts,
The whole earth is full of His glory."

And the foundations of the thresholds trembled at the voice of him who called out, while the temple was filling with smoke. Then I said,

"Woe is me, for I am ruined!
Because I am a man of unclean lips,
And I live among a people of unclean lips;
For my eyes have seen the King, the Lord of hosts."

Then one of the seraphim flew to me with a burning coal in his hand, which he had taken from the altar with tongs. He touched my mouth with it and said, "Behold, this has touched your lips; and your iniquity is taken away and your sin is forgiven" (Isaiah 6:1-7).

Activation #5: Engage the fiery altar

So now we are going to lie on that altar and let the Seraphim do their surgery with the fire of God's presence. Scan the QR code (right) or use the link on the resources webpage to listen to the audio recording, or read the text below.

Sometimes it feels as if you get ruined when you engage in these things. If you feel that you are undone, you can trust the Father. It is best just to lie there and be undone and allow Him to heal you.

Close your eyes, relax. By faith, choose to engage the altar.

Think of an altar, and think of the burning coals.
Just picture that in your imagination.
Picture the fire.

Then, by faith, because heaven is open, you can step into that place within the temple where the fiery altar is.
Ask Jesus to help you get on the altar.

As you lay on the altar,
ask the Father to reveal any hard areas in your heart,
any stony areas in your heart, any bad memories,
any broken, damaged, fragmented areas.

Ask Him to show you.
It may come as a memory, a thought,
or just an impression of something.
Just take the time to allow Him to unveil anything
that He wants to do heart surgery on.

Give Him permission.
Choose to open your heart to Him, to His love.
Ask Him to do that open-heart surgery
to remove, to heal, to restore;
to pour on His healing balm;
to bring you into wholeness.

Stay there as long as you need.

6. God is Love

So what is the Father really like? Because if we are going to enter into a relationship with Him, we will want to know what He is really like.

You can only know what someone is really like by spending quality time with them. I could say I knew the Queen of England, but I only knew about her from seeing footage of her carrying out her public duties on the TV, or from fictitious dramatisations of her life like *The Crown*. I did not know her and I never met her. I know about her, but even some of what I think I know about her may not be true.

Not as I thought

So we need to meet the Father to really know what He is like; and what I discovered was that He was not as I thought. The more I have got to know Him, the less He turns out to be as I thought. And that is a good thing, because He is so much better.

The Father is not at all who religion and culture have made Him out to be: each in their own way have misunderstood and therefore misrepresented Him. The Father is not an old man with a beard, a Santa Claus figure; and He is not the Old Testament angry God somewhere up there, who needs to be appeased with animal sacrifices. That is how He is often portrayed but He is not like that.

The Father is not watching, waiting for us to get it wrong, so He can punish us. That again is a view of God that makes people afraid of getting close to Him because they are fearful that He will punish them if they don't get it perfectly right. The Father is not the angry face of a two-faced god of which the good-natured side is Jesus. They are both exactly the same: love. The Father is not some cosmic child abuser who killed Jesus, His Son, to satisfy His anger and wrath. Religion has painted Him that way but He is not like that.

When we meet Him He will challenge some of the ideas we have, some of those constructs in our mind. The Father is not a torturer who will be tormenting vast numbers of His children forever because they did not do things the way He wanted. The Father is not a parent who abandons, disinherits and disowns His children if they ignore Him and go off track. He is not like that. The Father is not a parent who turned his back on Jesus on the cross either, which is again a religious tradition; He went through it with Him:

... namely, that God was in Christ reconciling the world [Greek kosmos] to Himself, not counting their trespasses against them, and He has committed to us the word of reconciliation (2 Corinthians 5:19).

God was in Christ, not separated from Him.

The Father is not a parent who has favourites amongst His children. He has not chosen some to be with Him and others to be separated from Him and punished forever. That is not Him, but nor is He some cosmic heavenly sugar daddy, who we can manipulate to give us what we want by trying to please Him or appease Him, or even by throwing tantrums around Him.

So we have got a whole lot of things wrong really, which God wants to change our thinking about. The reality is that He loves us, so He will only allow what is going on to be used for our good. Now that even means He allows us to make choices about our own life, and some of the consequences come out of our own choices, but He will not allow those consequences to stop us coming into the fullness of our sonship. We can never do anything that is unredeemable because Jesus has dealt with everything on the cross.

Like Jesus

Therefore, as we engage the Father, it is probably going to stretch our understanding and our experience and what we may have believed in the past. We can now see the Father, if we can see Jesus, the Son, who is His express image and likeness, and we can come to the Father for ourselves through Jesus, who is the door, and who brings us to the Father.

So when I engage the Father in heaven, and when I engage Him here at times, what I actually see is Jesus. I know it is not Jesus, because the fragrance, the frequency and the voice of the Father are different from Jesus, but His appearance is like Jesus. Not Jesus who is a little bit older, with a bit of grey in His beard or anything like that: all I can say is, He is like Jesus.

You need to find what He is like for yourself because He may well appear differently to you, but do not try to picture Him according to some illustrated Children's Bible or comic book view of what He is like, allow him to show you. That might well be more of an emotional experience than an image. Obviously we do not want an image that we try to worship, because that is idolatry: we want a relationship. It is the emotional relationship which is the key when we are engaging the Father, not just what He looks like. He wants to reveal Himself to us in love so that we can experience Him.

So the Father is fully represented in and by His Son, and is a loving, caring, compassionate Dad, who deeply desires all His children to be in an intimate love relationship with Him. That is His passion and He is at work in our lives all the time to seek to bring us into that relationship. Unfortunately, many of us have resisted or been unaware of that because of our conditioning.

A loving parent

God desires as our Father to constantly bless us: we are the apple of His eye and the treasure of His heart. When He looks at you, He is not looking at you the way you look at yourself or the way anyone else looks at you. When He looks at you He sees His original intention for you.

He is a loving parent who will never force His children to do anything. Sometimes people present it that God is sovereign and His sovereignty will be outworked whether we like it or not. Well, He is sovereign but not in that hyper-Calvinistic way: we are involved in the process. We have been given free will; we have been given the choice. And He does not force our choice. He does sometimes discipline us by allowing the consequences of our choices, to help us not to make the same poor choices over again, but He does not punish us for getting it wrong. Discipline is not the same as punishment. Discipline is discipleship, it is training and correction: it is intended to help us, not penalise us. According to Romans 2:4, He is patient, tolerant and kind. He is waiting with a joyful anticipation for our return to the fullness of relationship with Him: just like the father with the prodigal son, He is waiting, looking for us, and He will run to meet us.

So the Father has a love for all His children that will never end, will never fail and never give up; and He can never be separated from His children. That is very different from the picture that religion paints. Religion creates a separation in which God cannot look at you because you are dirty and unclean and a sinner. You are not a sinner, you are a saint. I am a new creation in Christ, and so are you. I do not think of myself as a sinner and therefore I do not anticipate sinning; and if I do make a wrong choice then He is there to redeem it, restore me and make me whole, and cleanse me from anything that is going to affect my relationship with Him.

God the Father is passionate about all of us. He is patiently working and waiting for all of us to return to that intimate love relationship with Him and doing whatever He can to help us. Sometimes we get caught up with what is going on around us or in our own feelings and emotions and fail to notice what He is doing. But the Father is working in every situation to constantly enable all our choices, in all our decisions, even the worst and most stupid of them, to produce something good; and He has even woven those things into the fulfilment of His heart's desire. It is not all fate; it is not all just going to happen. We really are a part of the process but He is not going to give up on bringing us into the fullest expression of that parent and child relationship.

In the mind of God

One time when I engaged in the heart of God, just enjoying being there and being loved, He said "I want to take you into My mind." I thought, "Wow! I'm going to be in among the firing neurons of the creativity of God! This is going to be amazing!"

But actually He took me into a conversation. I kept hearing my name in the conversation, which got my attention, and I began to realise that the mind of God is continually communicating in all these things because He desires to connect with all of us, all of the time. He is constantly reconnecting and re-correcting us to make sure we can still follow the path that He has set out for us. Even if we have gone off into some twisty side track, He is at work to bring us back; and He will even use the side track to be part of the story, because remember, He is in the 'now' – events are not past or present or future for Him, everything is in the 'now'.

He said, "I want to give you a glimpse of how that works." And all of a sudden I was sensing His connection to everyone who has ever existed and ever will exist, and that He is at work to bring good out of every thought, every choice and every decision they make. Now the latest estimate is that around one hundred and seventeen billion people have existed up to this point and I'm sure there are a lot more yet to be born but who are already there in the heart of God.

That experience so challenged me about how I look at people and how I find it so easy to judge people. He is looking at people with completely different eyes, the eyes of love, and it changed how I started to see people too. I had to see them through the eyes of love. So when I was frustrated because they were making foolish decisions over and over again, or not getting it when I thought it was obvious, then God would remind me, "That is not how I see people, and I am not frustrated with anybody. I love everybody and I am at work bringing that love into their lives and working that love to bring good out of everything for them."

My loving Dad

So there is really nothing you can do that will ever stop God loving you. Nothing could make Him love you any more, or any less. His love for you is full and complete. What we have to do is come into the knowledge of that love by experience.

We may fear God in the sense of respecting Him, but we do not need to be afraid of Him. Religion makes people afraid of God, afraid to come into that level of intimacy, thinking "What if He sees this?" Well, whatever it is, He already sees it and He is already at work in you to correct it and help you through it, all the time.

This is what the Father is like. He is my Dad. He is always available. He is never too busy for me. He never leaves me, always wants the best for me, is always interested in me, and always welcomes me into His open arms of love. My loving Dad is the most wonderful, faithful, trustworthy, patient, kind, good, joyful, peaceful, fun-loving, awesome Father, who is always sharing His heart and thoughts with me.

He has already predestined each one of us to be adopted as His children. He has already chosen us to be face to face with Him in blameless innocence. This is already being worked out but we choose when it happens, He does not force it upon us, and we can resist it for as long as we want. But when we start to get little glimpses of it, He starts to draw us in to engage His arms of love.

I love being with Him. Most of my cognitive engagements with God in heaven are actually with the Father. I used to hang out with Jesus a lot, I used to engage with the Holy Spirit a lot, but now most of the time I want to talk to the Father because He is fathering me into my sonship. He is your Dad too, and He wants us all to know this intimacy.

Arguments

A few years ago, we published a blog post called 'The Hell Delusion,' and found ourselves engaging with people who strongly disagreed with some of the things we were saying. It is people whose hearts are open, who are on their journey, that I really want to connect with us and with what we are saying, because it may be of help to them. So now I legislate for protection over what we are saying so that those who are not open to it do not even see or hear it.

But back then I was talking to the Father about it and He said "Son, do not be concerned with the arguments of those who do not know Me face to face." So that is one of the questions I ask people when they put forward some sort of theological doctrinal position to disprove my experiences with God. For me, someone else's argument is never going to disprove my experience and encounter but I do not want to be deliberately confrontational. So if someone says to me, 'This is the truth, and what you are saying is not true' then my question would be, "Where did you get that truth from? Did God give you that truth face to face? Did He speak that truth to you or tell you that was the truth? Or have you got it through some other teacher, some other system, some theology book or YouTube video, or whatever? No one has ever told me that God gave them that face to face. A face to face encounter with God beats a theology and a doctrine about Him every day of the week.

And He went on to say, "And with all the deceptions of those who are confirmationally biased because they have never allowed Me to deconstruct their minds, some people will always believe what they have always believed. Everything they encounter will always confirm what they believe, because they are not open to see anything different."

I have always tried to remain open. God has changed what I believe many times, from being in the Methodist Church, to being in the Brethren Church, to then getting baptised in the Spirit in the Brethren Church (which was quite a shock for people there, and for me), so I realise that I need to hold lightly to what I believe, because God is the truth, not my beliefs about Him. He can speak the truth: He is the truth and my engagement with Him will reveal the truth, which will probably expose many things I thought were true as not being true at all.

I have always been very passionate about what I believe, until I do not believe it anymore; because I am open for Him to change it, however passionate I may have been about it. A lot of things I just believed because it was the system of belief of the denomination or stream I was in, but now my experiences have deconstructed those beliefs.

I realise that people are on their own journey, so I am not going to argue with them or try to debate it. You can never win an argument when someone is trying to prove you wrong. But I love people and I want God to break in and reveal Himself to them the way He has revealed Himself to me. In fact I want them to go far beyond the tiny fraction I have experienced of our infinite God. Still, that fraction is amazing and wonderful, and I feel that I live in a blissful bubble of love all the time, no matter what is going on with me or around me. I am loved, I know I am loved, I know I am accepted.

Expressions of love

God said to me, "Once you have been in the circle of the dance, there is only one conclusion: that is love. And what does 1 Corinthians 13 say about love? That it torments and punishes? No. That love is kind and bears all things." He wants to unveil His nature as love.

Love is patient, love is kind and is not jealous; love does not brag and is not arrogant, does not act unbecomingly; it does not seek its own, is not provoked, does not take into account a wrong suffered, does not rejoice in unrighteousness, but rejoices with the truth; bears all things, believes all things, hopes all things, endures all things (1 Corinthians 13:4-7).

Those 'all things,' by the way, are the 'all things' that God wants to restore in the restoration of all things.

This is not about us looking at anyone else to point the finger and say "You're not very loving." It is about us looking in the mirror of that passage and saying "Do I see myself reflected in that? Am I loving? Am I easily provoked? Am I keeping account of wrongs? We cannot love that way unless we know love as a person, not a theory or a concept.

And God would not expect us to carry those characteristics if He did not. So He is not easily provoked (in fact He is never provoked at all) and He does not take into account any wrong suffered. When we start to look at that, it begins to change how we see God and how we encounter Him. That passage continues:

Love never fails; but if there are gifts of prophecy, they will be done away with; if there are tongues, they will cease; if there is knowledge, it will be done away with (1 Corinthians 13:8).

Our knowledge will be done away with but His love never fails. So no matter what you do, no matter where you are, love does not fail. That means that God does not fail; God does not give up on you, in fact He will never give up on you. Do we believe that? Is that our experience? Here is the same passage in The Mirror Bible:

Love is large in being passionate about life and relentlessly patient in bearing the offenses and injuries of others with kindness. Love is completely content and strives for nothing. Love has no desire to make others feel inferior and has no need to sing its own praises. Love is predictable and does not behave out of character. Love is not ambitious. Love is not spiteful and gets no mileage out of another's mistakes. Love sees no joy in injustice. Love's delight is in everything that truth celebrates. Love is a fortress where everyone feels protected rather than exposed. Love's persuasion is persistent. Love believes. Love never loses hope and always remains constant in contradiction. Love never loses its altitude. Prophecies will cease. Tongues will pause. The quest for knowledge will be inappropriate when perfection is grasped (1 Corinthians 13:4-8 Mirror).

God does not change or behave out of character. He is not going to wake up tomorrow morning angry or in a bad mood; He is always smiling, His countenance is always fair over all of us. God has made us as His children so He does not want us to feel inferior about our sonship.

God will never lose hope in you. You may have lost hope in yourself; you may have felt disillusioned; you may have felt disappointed if things have not worked out the way you thought, or if His promises seem out of reach. God never loses hope: He looks at you and sees you the way He created you to be. When we start to look into that mirror and see that too, it begins to change us.

Who will separate us from the love of Christ? Will tribulation, or distress, or persecution, or famine, or nakedness, or peril, or sword? ... But in all these things we overwhelmingly conquer through Him who loved us. For I am convinced that neither death, nor life, nor angels, nor principalities, nor things present, nor things to come, nor powers, nor height, nor depth, nor any other created thing, will be able to separate us from the love of God, which is in Christ Jesus our Lord (Romans 8:35, 37-39).

No matter what you do, you cannot separate yourself from God's love. But you can fail to experience it – and God wants you to experience it in practice, not in theory. This is what He said:

"Son, anything that contradicts love is a contradiction of My character; anything that presents Me as anything other than love is a perversion of the truth; any representation of Me that is not love is a lie. I am spirit, light, and a consuming fire – and above all, love. Therefore love is spirit, light and a consuming fire. Any characteristics that I have, like righteousness and justice, and yes, anger and wrath, are full representations of love. Love is always patient, kind and good; therefore all My judgments, all My justice, all My anger and all My wrath must be – and are – fully love, without any contradiction."

Our understanding of judgment, justice, anger and wrath is wrong if it does not equate to love. So when we think of those words we need to be really careful that we do not interpret them through our own understanding, through what we think they mean, because that will not be the way God is.

"All of those things are expressions of love. All of My characteristics are restorative not retroactive or punitive. I discipline and disciple my children, not punish them, and I will never be separated from them."

Love is always patient, kind and good. I want to encourage you to take those words and allow them to form in your thinking. Do not think of them as just words: they are living words, they are the truth. Now take that and experience it; allow it to bring truth to you.

Repentance, confession and judgment

Or do you think lightly of the riches of His kindness and tolerance and patience, not knowing that the kindness of God leads you to repentance? (Romans 2:4).

Our understanding of repentance needs to be renewed from that light of God's love. Repentance is not us being sorry and making amends for all the things we do wrong, repentance is agreeing with what God says about us. The Greek word is *metanoia*, which literally means 'with mind', in other words, in agreement with God's mind. When I am out of agreement with God's mind, repentance means that I come into agreement with God's mind. I let God's mind inform what the truth is, reveal that truth to me; I agree with it and then I am changed by it. I experience a radical shift in my thinking: away from what I used to think, into now thinking the way God thinks about me. Paul continues:

But because of your stubbornness and unrepentant heart you are storing up wrath for yourself in the day of wrath and revelation of the righteous judgment of God (Romans 2:5).

71

So how does that make us feel? If we see it through the lens of love, then we will realise that it is going to be a good thing for us, not bad. However, if we read that with a typical religious mindset of what God is like, we think "Oh no, if I'm stubborn and won't change my mind then God is going to be mad at me and I'm going to be punished." No, what God is doing when we are stubborn and resistant is working in us to reveal the truth so that we will come into agreement with it. He is not looking to punish us or to try to get us to change our mind because we are afraid of what God is going to do to us. The word translated 'wrath', Greek *orge*, can equally well be translated 'passion'. So God passionately wants to engage us, and there is a day coming for all of us (and some of us are already living this) when that desire for relational engagement can be outworked in our daily life, because of the revelation of the righteous judgment of God.

What was God's righteous judgment? The cross. And what did God do on the cross? He dealt with every accusation and every decree that could ever be used against us and nailed it to the cross. So, as we saw earlier in this chapter, God was in Christ reconciling the whole cosmos to himself, not counting their sin (which is their lost identity and not knowing their sonship) against them (see 2 Corinthians 5:19). If He is not holding it against us, why do we hold it against ourselves and why do we hold it against other people? So what is the verdict pronounced by God's righteous judgment? Not guilty! He has already forgiven us.

If we confess our sins, He is faithful and righteous to forgive us our sins and to cleanse us from all unrighteousness (1 John 1:9).

Saying, "I'm really sorry, I was wrong" is not what the word 'confess' means in this context. The concept of confession is as misunderstood as repentance: 'to confess' means 'to say with'. If we confess (agree and say the same thing as God) that our sins are forgiven, then we live in a cleansed state of righteousness. This kind of confession is not like in the legal system where the guilty party makes a confession to a crime, it is agreeing, confessing what God says is true.

72

But religion will always have us focus on how bad we are, not on the fact that He has made us righteous. God says I am forgiven, so if I continually live in the confession that I am forgiven, I no longer focus on sin: it is not something that determines how I behave, nor does it define me. I am no longer sin-conscious but righteousness-conscious.

God wants to reveal what we are really like, to unveil and bring us into the truth of the revelation of Him. This is what He said to me about all His righteous judgment:

"Yes, My passion is poured out in My righteous judgment which was first executed before the foundation of the world, re-enacted on the cross, and finally enacted in AD 70 at the end of the Old Covenant system."

I have gone into detail about what happened in AD 70 in my book *The Eschatology of the Restoration of all Things*[4]. What many evangelical believers traditionally view as prophecies still to happen in the future, God has in reality already fulfilled. So for example, if we are looking for a Great Tribulation still to come, the good news is that it has already happened, in AD 70. 'Realised eschatology' is a whole belief system which does not put everything off into the future but sees it all as having been fulfilled in the first century, so that then we can live in the blessing of that fulfilment today.

"All of My judgment is an expression of My love and is designed to allow the consequences of individual choice to bring all to true *metanoia* [true repentance]."

His love, His kindness, His tolerance and His patience will bring us to a true repentance, a change of heart and mind in which we agree with Him about ourselves. It is not that His fierce anger makes us afraid of Him, so that we had better say sorry, or else! He is not like that. There is no 'or else!' We only

---

[4] See eg.freedomarc.org/books for details of this and Mike's other books.

create our own 'or elses' which are the consequences of what we do.

Stronger than death

"I will fiercely defend the right of My children to choose; but I will fiercely enable good to come out of every choice. My love will never fail, never give up and will never allow My children to be separated from Me. My love is stronger than death and the grave." Just think about all of the possible implications of God saying, "My love is stronger than death."

Death was swallowed up in the victory which came about by the resurrection. All died in Adam: from Jesus' resurrection onwards, all will be made alive in Christ (see Romans 5:18). So everyone has now been made alive. That is why He is at work in everyone; that is why the Spirit has been poured out on everyone.

"Put me like a seal over your heart,
Like a seal on your arm.
For love is as strong as death,
Jealousy is as severe as Sheol;
Its flashes are flashes of fire,
The very flame of the Lord.
Many waters cannot quench love,
Nor will rivers overflow it;
If a man were to give all the riches of his house for love,
It would be utterly despised" (Song of Solomon 8:6-7).

I love that scripture. We sing it in a Misty Edwards song called "You Won't Relent" – and He really won't. He will not relent until He has it all, and He wants us lock, stock and barrel.

"Put me like a seal over your heart, like a seal on your arm," in other words "Let me engage your emotions and reveal love." Our arm is symbolic of what we do; so this is saying, "in all your works, let there be love." God is jealous (jealousy is not a bad thing when it is directed the right way). He is jealous for our relationship, jealous for our sonship, jealous for our being in intimacy with Him.

"Flashes of fire" because our God is a consuming fire. Fire does not actually destroy anything, it just changes its form. If you burn wood, you get ash and smoke, which still exist. And if we embrace the fire of God, it will change and transform us because that is what it is designed to do. In Greek, the word 'fire' is *'pyr'* or *'pur'*, which gives us words like 'purify' and 'purification.' His fire is an expression of His love, consuming in us everything which hinders us from experiencing His love.

"If a man were to give all the riches of his house for love, it would be utterly despised." We cannot buy it, it is given to us free. It is the nature of God Himself. However it comes, it is an expression of His very heart of love and He wants us to experience it.

7. Relational Intimacy

Circle of the dance

"Son, My deepest desire is that all My children will fully participate in the circle of the dance." That word in Greek is *perichoresis* and it is a description of the relationship of God as Father, Son and Spirit. The circle of the dance very aptly describes my experiences of being there.

"That is what it feels like to know My love in its most relational intimacy." That is God's desire: He wants us to know His love in his relational intimacy.

"I AM is calling all Our children to be fully restored to sonship, so that they can live loved, love living and live loving." This is really how God expressed to me how He wants me to live. He wants me to live loved. That means that I live my whole life from a perspective of being within the love of God and experiencing the intimacy of that passion and that fire for me. It is a seal on my heart and on my arm. I live in the bliss bubble of love because I know I am loved. I do not have to earn that love; I cannot do anything to stop that love; but I can really, really enjoy it!

And then I can love living. Life can sometimes feel like a drudgery and hard work but when you live loved you see life from a whole new perspective. It becomes an opportunity: an opportunity to experience the depth of God's love, deeper and deeper; an opportunity for us to see the world from His love perspective and so to love the world.

"For God so loved the world, that He gave His only begotten Son, that whoever believes in Him shall not perish, but have eternal life" (John 3:16).

We know this scripture very well, or we think we do. God so loved the world – but the world was not just people, because again the Greek word is *kosmos,* which includes everything He has created. So everything that He has created, He loves.

76

That will start to stretch us, once we realise that He wants to restore everything that He has created, because He loves it.

So when we live loved, we can love living and live loving. Our lives can become a reflection and a demonstration of that love to others. I am not perfect at it, but I am much better than I was because I am discovering more and more each day what it is to live loved, more and more what it is to know the Father who is love, and to experience and live within that love so that I can live in a more loving way. I want to create an atmosphere of love around me. I want people to engage me and feel loved, feel accepted and feel affirmed.

You cannot get your affirmation and acceptance from me, and no matter who you try to get it from, even your spouse, they can never give you what God can give you. So we each need to get that love, affirmation and acceptance from engaging in intimacy with our Father. Then we give it to others, not as a substitute for God but to express the same quality of love that we have received. Love is about giving: God so loved that He gave, and so will we.

Arise and shine

"Creation itself is waiting for the revealing of the sons of love's light to arise and shine, with their glory fully restored."

God wants to restore us to the glory that we once had as His children. Just as Adam was clothed with glory, we can be clothed with glory: our spirit can be surrounding us and it is made of light. And creation itself is looking, waiting for us to be revealed, to be shining:

"Arise, shine; for your light has come,
And the glory of the Lord has risen upon you" (Isaiah 60:1).

The reason we are not seeing or doing all the things that Jesus did is that we are not radiating and shining love's light. That comes through love; it comes through outworking who we are in sonship. It does not come with learning new techniques to administer healing. The church is always coming up with

77

new methods and models which become the latest fad. That could happen with the courts of heaven if it gets turned into just another prayer system: people will not then be going into heaven, into a real court, they will just be going through the motions as a formula, without the power. Because that is what we do, we take everything that God gives us and try to operate it in our own understanding, which takes all the life out of it. God wants to do everything in relationship with us, not give us a formula.

He desires to restore us to our glory as sons of light. If we have not experienced God in this light and we do not know the deepest levels of His love, it is time to encounter that love. He wants us to encounter love; He wants us to experience it.

He said this to me. "Son, sonship is the only priority you need to set. When My children begin to take their heavenly places as sons then they will be able to discern My heart's deepest desire, which is the purity of relationship that will be experienced within the restoration of all My sons who arise."

Love

There are just some things that we cannot get unless we go into His presence, into where He is. Yes, it is great when He comes here and meets with us but there are some things we have to experience in His realm, for the atmosphere of that realm to change us. He wants us to come into that realm.

"Son, love is not just the essence of who I am but is to be the essence of who you are. If you really want the world to know Me they need to see love in action. When My children truly know Me they will love one another and the world they are part of and responsible for."

We have been given responsibility for creation. Adam's mandate for creation was to establish fruitfulness, to multiply, to increase, to overcome and to rule. We still have that same responsibility to overcome and rule.

"Religion in all its forms cannot truly represent love because it is not relational and therefore cannot reveal My true nature to the world. Love is not love if it is not otherly because love is not just about receiving, it is primarily about giving. Love Me with all your being, and then you will be able to love yourself and others – but you can only love Me through relationship, not concepts. You must know Me to love Me. Relationship cannot be theoretical it must be the real interaction that occurs between us."

So often we conceptualize everything and lose the relational heart of it, and God wants to bring the relational back into it. These are some of the conversations I have with God: He talks to me and tells me all kinds of things. Sometimes I understand what He is saying and other times not. Then I have to go and ask Him about it, because that takes me back into relationship. If I try to figure it out on my own it is not relational. I suspect He often says things deliberately to cause me to go back to Him and to relate with Him.

"I know you and I know everything about you now, and I love you as I love all My children. Relationship was never meant to be one way. We are pure relationship in the dance of I AM, and we desire that all our children experience I AM in intimacy within us, within you."

How do we experience intimacy with Him within us and us within Him? It sounds complicated and mixed up if you try to figure it out with your intellect, because it is not designed to be figured out but to be experienced in relationship with Him.

Deep calls

"Son, that is why deep is calling to deep. It is the call to know love in its purest essence without agenda or need. I AM is calling like the sound of many waters, across all dimensions of time and space, to all the broken hearts and parts to come back to the wholeness only found in the oneness of I AM."

God wants us to be whole: that is what *shalom*, peace, really is: it is wholeness. There are many waterfalls in heaven but

79

there is one particular waterfall under which I have stood and had some really amazing encounters. This is what God said:

"The waterfall has many purposes but mostly it is to express love in such a way that it draws My children back to My heart as Father. I am calling you to come deeper, My children, into the depths of My loving heart. Come back to the beginning in face to face innocence; and see yourself the way I AM sees you, and you will truly know yourself as My sons."

Deep calls to deep at the sound of Your waterfalls;
All Your breakers and Your waves have rolled over me
(Psalm 42:7).

This verse is a description of what God is wanting us to experience. Jesus experienced those breakers and waves on the cross – I do not mean all the terrible pain and torture which He had to endure, but over all that, the love of His Father, waves of love continually breaking over Him.

The Father wants to meet us and take us deeper into Himself, to reveal Himself to us at an even deeper level, beyond our understanding: to pure bliss, pure intimacy and relationship. God wants us to experience the waterfall of His presence. The sound of that waterfall is powerful and all-encompassing. It contains all the frequencies we can hear, from the very high to the very low. Something begins to vibrate in you and causes you to come into agreement with the sound of His voice, cascading down over you and absolutely empowering you and fashioning you with its presence.

Activation #6: The waterfall

So I encourage you now to close your eyes and hear the sound of it. Let this become an experience that you actually step into. You can find both the audio version and the waterfall sound on the download page.

By faith take a step through the open realm of heaven and ask Jesus to take you to the waterfall cascading down with the river of life.

Let Jesus take you to stand under the waterfall of the Father's love.
Let that love cascade over your whole being.

Let the sound of His voice vibrate within you.
Let it energise you, activate you,
so that you can fully experience the fullness of His life,
not just for you but for others and for all creation.

Hear the sound of His voice, the sound of many waters.
Let His voice speak love into your heart to bring healing and wholeness, calling you out of brokenness
into restored relationship, health and blessing.

Let your spirit resonate with the truth of His life.

That first time I experienced this, I was not feeling the love of God for myself (although I know that God loves me): rather it gave me a sense of His love for creation, for the cosmos, drawing me to go beyond and deeper; a sense of how much God loves everything and how much He wants to motivate me to see everything from His perspective. It was a really intense encounter. Sometimes you just know such encounters will be transformatory.

We had a meeting that same evening. I shared all of this and said "Let's go and engage the waterfall" because I really wanted to go back there! So we did. I do not know what other people were experiencing but I was experiencing an even deeper profound sense of the love of God coming and going over me. I felt connected to people who were suffering from not knowing the love of God, from being rejected, being abused and hurt. I felt their pain and I felt love for them, I felt the heart of God for them. I was caught up in this and thinking, "Wow, You love people so much" and how much we want to see people experience that love and be healed and made whole. There were tears in my eyes.

Then, all of a sudden, I felt the love of God for those who were the perpetrators, the victimisers and the abusers. His love for them is exactly the same as for the people they have abused and hurt. It so shocked me, because it is relatively easy to feel love for those who have been suffering, but what about those who are causing the suffering? What God revealed was that His love for everyone is the same. So again it changed the way I viewed people: it changed my perception and making judgments of people; it changed my heart. I realised just how much God's love really is for all that He has created, for everybody. God wants us all to experience that for ourselves and to engage it.

"Son, this is love's agenda, where all things of the created order will be returned to relational connectedness within My unity."

Our restored sonship affects the created order itself. So the question is, will we willingly engage in love's agenda, which is found in relationship with Him? He wants us to engage that and experience it and go beyond where we presently are with it: to receive from Him the motivation of His heart, to be moved with what moves Him, to be moved with love and compassion, to be moved to experience something deeper and deeper of His love.

He wants us to realise that creation is groaning; and its groaning is for reconciliation and restoration; it is groaning in bondage because it has lost its connectedness with us. And God wants to restore us, so that we can see creation restored; to see everything brought back into God's original intention and original condition. We are the sons of God. Creation is for us, so we are responsible for it. Think about the so-called 'green agenda': there are people out there who may not know God but are catching some of the heart of God for creation. They do not know that is what it is, or where it is coming from, but it is a cause which resonates with them. Perhaps they do have hurts and find it cathartic to love the natural world when they are hurt themselves, but the reality is that they are catching the heart of God, His love of creation and

His love for them; because He wants us all to experience that love and engage that love for ourselves.

When we can truly live loved, then we will love this life that He has given us; and we will live that life, loving everyone and everything in it, bringing restoration to all things relationally. If we are not reconciled with people, we need to allow the love of God to move us to reconciliation as much as is possible from our side. Some people may not be reconciled with us but we can still be reconciled towards them, just as God has reconciled all of creation to Himself. He wants everyone to know what He has already done: we outwork our sonship responsibility towards creation by living loved, in relationship with God, in such a way that people catch it, that people want it, that they see something in us and feel something about us, and realise that what they are picking up from us is coming from Love Himself.

A guided tour of heaven

Therefore let us draw near with confidence to the throne of grace, so that we may receive mercy and find grace to help in time of need (Hebrews 4:16).

As we have mentioned, the throne of grace is an actual place you can go in the realms of heaven. We all have the resources of heaven available to us just like Jesus: He was able to access everything in the realms of heaven and so do we.

We can engage the River of Life which is flowing from the throne of God. It is the essence of the life of God and we can experience it. We can dive in and swim in the river; the river can flow in us; we can drink that river; we can even breathe in the river because it is not H_2O, it is the life of God that is designed for us. There are waterfalls, as we have experienced already. There are all sorts of things in the river, it is a great place to be!

The river flows through the Father's garden, another beautiful place we can enjoy. The Tree of Life grows along its banks; it is fantastic to eat the fruit of the tree of life, which is in season

83

all the time. It is for us to eat, not just to have a familiar passage in Revelation that we read and think, "Oh, that's nice!" It is there for us to engage.

As we step into Eden we can ask Jesus or ask the Father to take us to engage in some of those wonderful places and things. Ask Him to take you on a trip to show you some of the things in Eden. If you are used to engaging in heaven, then by all means go wherever you feel you want to go; but if you are not, then ask for a guided tour... but not from me! I could only take you to the places that I know how to go to. God Himself can take you wherever you personally need to go. I am going to come on this tour myself, but it is going to be led by Jesus, by the Father or by the Holy Spirit. They will take you anywhere They want to.

We have a door within our spirit we call our first love gate. Jesus is knocking at the door within our spirit and we have the choice whether we open that door or not. When we do open the door we have access not just for the Father, Son and Spirit to come to us but for us to go back through that door, because it is like a wormhole into another realm, another dimension.

When I first started engaging in my spirit, I was just captivated by God. I mean, to see the face of God, to look into His eyes and to be embraced by the Father or Jesus was amazing. I loved that, so I was not looking around me for anything more. Then when I started to do activations with other people, I decided that, rather than get caught up in the activation, it would be better to observe, so that I could help others. So then I looked into my spirit and I realised my spirit was in the form of a mountain, which made sense because I am a mountain, I am a place of authority.

One time we did an activation with a group here and afterwards we were feeding back what had happened. One person said she had gone back through the door. Why had I not thought of that? I knew I was able to access heaven by going in through the 'door standing open in heaven' which John described in Revelation 4:1 so I had never thought to access it through my own spirit. Our own spirit gives direct access into the garden, through relationship. The other access we have, governmentally, is through the realms of the kingdom of God, the kingdom of heaven, and heaven; and into the tabernacle through the gateway of the Way, the Truth and the Life. There is a process and progression to follow in government, which we will come to in due course, but here in the intimacy of relationship there are no barriers.

Activation #7: The River of Life

So I started to go back through the gate and I found myself immediately by the River of Life. Let's do that now.

Close your eyes and begin to think of a door, with the door handle on your side. If you find it hard to picture a door, maybe think of one that you are familiar with, such as your own front door.

As you picture it,
let that form a doorway for you to step through.

So by faith, reach out, open the door,
and wait for the presence of God to come in and embrace you.

Let the Father embrace you.
Feel His presence; feel His love.

And then, just by choice, ask the Father to take you back through the door into Eden.

As you step through the door, you step through a veil, and you are transported into the realm of Eden.

There is the River of Life.

Now ask the Father to show you whatever you need to experience...

[For me, I am just going to get in the River of Life. I am going to enjoy myself and float around, and just experience that life surrounding me, flowing through me, and flowing in me...]

Beyond the river are the waterfalls cascading down which we engaged with earlier. You can choose to engage there. You can float up a waterfall in the realms of heaven, there is no gravity; so you can float up, or you can float down.

If you have floated up, maybe the Father will take you the scenic route, walking along the pathway, enjoying the awesomeness of the colours, fragrances and frequencies of heaven.

If you follow that path, you come to a bridge; and you can cross over into the Father's garden; or you can carry on up the waterfalls and come to the Tree of Life.

If He takes you into His garden, which is the most beautiful expression of paradise, just rest – it is the place of most perfect rest.

Again, there are waterfalls in the garden; there is a beautiful pool which will take you into some deep things if you dive in there.

If you keep following the river, you will end up engaging the Tree of Life, with beautiful fruits and scrolls which you can take and eat.

(In the realms of heaven, when you receive something such as a fruit, or a gemstone, or a scroll, mostly you can eat them and take them into yourself, absorb their goodness and allow their revelation to unveil in you.)

Maybe the Father will take you to the throne of grace and lift you up onto His lap. You can place your head on His breast and feel the rhythm of His heart; and you can just offload everything onto Him and come to that place of perfect rest.

Wherever He takes you, go with it.

When I first started engaging this, I would spend hours there. This is just a taster, an encouragement for you to pursue the same thing. Every time you open that door you can engage the presence of God within and you can step back through that door.

Sometimes, the desire of your heart will take you there. If you really set the desire of your heart on something, then God opens that up for you to engage. I desired to engage the waterfalls because waterfalls are something I have always liked. I have seen quite a few, been close to them, and really felt the energy just from a natural waterfall, so I always wanted to go to waterfalls in heaven.

And then after a while I discovered that there were things behind the waterfall that I never knew were there. I found a cave behind the waterfall and I went in and met Enoch. He gave me some things to do, so I avoided going back there for a while! 'Quests,' he called them. Now I am a *Lord of the Rings* type of person so quests and adventures are all part of my makeup. As a child I loved adventures and would go out and explore. God made me that way, and He uses the way He made me to engage in things. Some people find rooms attractive and they love to go into rooms in heaven, like the library room, or the record room; I have been in those places but they don't hold the same sort of attraction for me as a garden, or a waterfall, or a beautiful river. Those are the kinds of places I generally choose to engage and I spend time – sometimes hours – in each place.

Heavenly time

Time functions in the realms of heaven differently to how it does here. Besides that, there are different realms of heaven, and the closer you get to God Himself, the faster the speed of light. In this realm we operate in created light; but heaven is made of creative light and our spirits are creative light. The closer we get to God, the closer we get to the optimum speed of light, so everything then becomes 'now.'

The Kingdom of God realm, where our mountains are and where the court of accusation is, that seems to operate just a little faster than this realm. It is always before this realm, so the things that are coming out of that realm you would call prophetic, because they have not yet happened here but are established and decreed there so that they can happen here.

But then the Kingdom of Heaven realm seems to be quite a bit faster again, so you can be there an hour and it feels like a day. Consciously you may not be able to receive everything, but actually you are receiving a lot more than an hour's worth! When I first engaged in heaven, I had experiences which were so profound that they could not have happened in the hour that I was there physically. So if we spend five minutes engaging, do not think that five minutes is not worth having – sometimes five minutes can give you a lifetime's worth of change as you begin to outwork what you have received.

Though I do like to spend as much time as possible engaging! I used to spend hours just being in the Father's garden, floating there, being at rest. He was teaching me to stop trying to actively do things and just be there with Him, at peace. Eventually I learned to be part of the atmosphere of that place because it felt like I was one with it, just becoming one with His love. As I was there one day, I was floating and I felt totally weightless; I had no sense of feeling and it was as if all the atoms of my whole being just exploded and I connected with the whole of creation. I felt the groan and the disharmony, but I also felt the heart of God for it. I felt responsible, in a sense, that "I have a part to play in this." I actually began to connect to the areas of creation that Eve had a mandate to engage with, just because I connected to it in a way which I could never have done otherwise.

I used to make up excuses to go to the throne of grace just because I loved sitting on the Father's lap. But I found that He loves it too when I am there, enjoying His presence. So

88

sometimes I go because I have things I would like help with (all I do is just offload them, and He is at work while I am at rest) and sometimes I go just because I enjoy being in His presence.

It is when we rest, when we stop trying to do it all ourselves, that we allow Him to do the things that we could never do – or to give us the wisdom, insight and grace to be able to do them in the relationship of sonship.

Spirit, soul and body

Sonship is not just about having a restored soul and becoming whole, as wonderful as that is; it is amazing to come into wholeness, and the more integrated and whole I become, the more I feel loved (and the more I sense that love, because nothing is hindering it or blocking it). I have gone through some pretty deep experiences to bring me to that point, it did not happen in an instant.

One of those experiences dealt with my soul, separating my soul and spirit and reintegrating them, so that I would be free to live in dual realms and not tethered to the earth. Another was a four-month process in which God took me through a whole relational experience of being prepared for marriage to Him (we talk about being the Bride of Christ, but God want us to be husband and wife, not waiting to consummate our relationship sometime in the future). That involved dealing with behaviours, motives and attitudes and eventually the core issue of me being in control and needing to know what was going on. When my soul knew what God was doing, I felt safe and secure; and my identity was coming from knowing. I did not realise that, but He did. He wanted to take me into the realms beyond the Kingdom of God but He could not trust me with that because I would have used those experiences to validate who I am.

It was the hardest four months of my life, but the best four months in some ways because eventually, after the four months, I surrendered. I gave up, and immediately my soul was completely separated from independence and was integrated with my soul and spirit. Before that, I could only step into heaven and step out again because my soul would not let my spirit stay there. I was never flowing out of heaven: I was always stepping in, experiencing something, stepping back out and trying to outwork that experience through my own understanding. So God took me through this process and from that day on, my spirit has been in the realms of heaven continually.

So as I say, having a restored soul is amazing, but what I want to encourage you is that that restored soul brings a balance between spirit, soul and body; it brings a freedom for the spirit to be in the realms of heaven, living in dual (or multiple) realms, and yet be completely connected to the soul. One of the reasons why I can answer a lot of the questions people ask me is that my spirit is in heaven and that revelation is flowing from there to here. The scientific term is 'quantum entanglement' – it describes how two things can be in separate places, divided by millions of miles, or in a different dimension, and still be completely connected.

So my soul now comes into agreement with my spirit. I am resonating with God, vibrating at His frequency; and my soul begins to vibrate at the same frequency. That means that I am instantly in agreement and in cooperation rather than needing to go through a process each time. Once that was happening I was free to go 'beyond beyond.'

In the Father

Sonship is about being in the Father and the Father being in us. It goes beyond just a relationship to being a position: we are in Him, He is in us. One result of this is that when we are in Him, we can be anywhere He is, as He is omnipresent throughout all dimensions of time and space. So I have gone back into time and seen things (because in the early days I was inquisitive to know how things worked). So for example, I stepped onto the timeline and went back to see how the pyramids were built. I had been to Egypt and visited the pyramids five or six times, been inside them, and every time I felt an energy. I know new age people talk about 'pyramid power' but actually there is energy in the pyramids because they are governmental – they are in the form of a mountain, representing authority. The New Jerusalem is also a pyramid, by the way, not a square or a cube. So I went back and saw that the Great Pyramid was not made by thousands of slaves, or by piling up sand; it was done through sound and light. They had the ability to lift and levitate heavy items, to cut stone and more besides.

I have not been back to do that kind of thing for quite a while now because I figure that if I need to know anything, God will show me. At that time it was my desire to know that led me into places but now it is His desire that leads me. Since I know that I am in the Father, and in Him I have access to anywhere that He wants me to go, I make myself available all the time, and particularly when I go to sleep at night.

One night I was engaging with the presence of God in the garden and I just said to Him, "I'm available for an adventure." I went to sleep and He took me (or I had access to go) into the past. Someone was praying, asking for healing because their child was dying, but this was in seventeen sixty-something in the middle of America somewhere. I just found myself there; I went to the door of the house and they let me in. I do not know what my spirit looked like to them, but they were seemingly open to me coming in. I prayed for the child, who was healed and restored, and I came back to the present.

I have always been interested in science fiction, and the paradoxes associated with time travel, so I thought "how does this work? How could I have gone back to the past?" Well, to Him it is not the past, it is all 'now'. So in the timeline, I had always prayed for that person, but I only became aware of it now, in my present. They were crying out and I was available so God used me. I have done that quite a few times now, and I know other people have also done it, because you are not limited by time or space when you are in Him. Sons get to be 'about the Father's business' (which I have come to understand is the restoration of all that He created), so we can do all sorts of adventurous things because we are in the Father and positioned in Him.

Wouldn't it be wonderful if our worship services were around the throne of God in heaven, and we were all there on the Father's business, being assigned all over time and space? That can happen if we are all open to engage these things and not limited by the restrictions of being earthbound.

Positioned, seated, enthroned

Sonship is about being positioned in the Father so that He can position us as His express image into creation. We are His sons, we are His representatives, so He wants to place us in positions where creation responds to us and we will bring restoration to it. That is why He is teaching us about sonship. It is not just about laying hands on someone and they will get well, that is something we are mandated to do in this realm anyway. It is far more significant and far-reaching than that.

Sonship is about being positioned seated and enthroned in heaven, so it is there that our governmental position can be manifested through our lives. When we are seated in heavenly places, we can administrate in heaven and outwork on the earth.

Sonship is then about being a gateway for the Father to touch the earth through our lives. Jesus said, "The Father who lives in Me does His work through me" (see John 14:10). The Father did not operate independently of Jesus, nor Jesus independently of the Father: they acted in total cooperation and relationship with one another. We want to get to that point where we are 'joined to the Lord and one spirit with Him' (see 1 Corinthians 6:17); where we cannot tell whether it is us doing something or the Spirit doing it – and it really does not matter either way. We are bringing heaven to earth, because we are one.

Sonship is about being a gateway for the Father to touch others. The way we do that is changing. It used to be that the

92

'man of power for the hour' would stand up at the front, prophesying over people, laying hands on everyone and knocking them flat on the floor. I have done that. What we want to do now instead is equip everyone to do what God is saying, rather than have one person do it on behalf of everyone else. That was the old 'mediator' model, and often it was like a blunderbuss or a shotgun approach: blast everything out there, tag it with 'in the name of Jesus' and hope that some of it would stick.

God wants us all to be equipped to release His love and power into other people's lives, and to do so because we actually see what is going on; then we can direct the flow of the grace of God to touch the precise areas that need healing. Most physical disorders are the result of emotional hurt and pain, so if you do not heal the emotions, the physical symptoms just keep returning. You need to get to the root of the issue – and it will be different every time.

So how do you do that? By reading the thoughts and intentions of people's hearts. Seeing into someone's DNA, into the fabric of their being, you can identify where trauma is trapped in cells, and where they are stuck and fragmented; not as some kind of magic party trick, but in order to bring healing as a precision instrument. It is one thing to get words of knowledge from the Holy Spirit, but what He really wants is to teach our spirit to function that way. If we can all be equipped to be like Jesus, to do the things Jesus did in the same way that He did them, then we will be able to go on to do the greater works as He promised we would (see John 14:22).

I asked Jesus one time how He knew what to do, and how He should do it. I had the idea that maybe He would go to the Father each morning and get a list, probably written on a scroll. And I thought it would be very specific: heal this blind person by spitting on the ground and making mud; heal this other one by speaking to them; and this one by touching their eyes. But that was not it at all – He just had the heart of the

Father to heal people that day and then, creatively, as a son, chose how to do it.

My mandate for the day is not a list of things I should do and how to do them. I am seated with Him in heaven, knowing His heart; and throughout the day I am continually connected to His heart, so I can always be where I need to be and do what I need to do, flowing in relationship with Him.

Everything always comes back to relationship. We tend to get into certain ways of thinking, ways of doing things, but God's way is always relational, not functional or structural – and in particular, not formulaic. We like to have a formula, but if a formula always worked we would not need a relationship. When we are in the heart of God, we can choose our reality. But I cannot assume that because I did something in a certain way one day, then I can do the same thing in the same way the next. God has not set it up that way, because He only works through relationship – He is one God in three persons, and relationship is at the core of His nature.

So sonship is about being involved in the restoration of all things back to God's original desire and design. That includes and begins with us: He wants us to be totally restored, made whole, our image conformed to His original pattern. But it goes beyond us into everything else He created. When you start to know the heart of God, you begin to feel how passionate He is about restoring everything. It is not just that eventually He will have the end agree with the beginning: He does not want anything to remain unrestored. I used to think Jesus would come back and suddenly He would make it all happen. As I engaged with God I realised that is not how it is going to be. Jesus is not going to do it. Who is going to do the restoring? God and us together in relationship. A Father and sons family business of restoration.

And what we think of as 'restoration' is only the beginning. Once all things are restored, then it can all continue to develop, released from the hiatus that we have been through for the last few thousand years, into what it will be (and was always intended to be). We need to go beyond Adam as sinless into what he would have become had he been perfected. We are all sons, but some of us are still infants, crawling or maybe toddling, or some may be walking; but God wants to mature us so that we can be part of the decision-making processes of heaven. He does not want to do things independently of us, He has chosen to include us in His government and without us His government is not complete. God is sovereign, but in His sovereignty He has chosen to work with us.

So when you read or hear about the courts of heaven, it is not all about doing court cases about accusations; most of it is about us participating in the assemblies and councils of God, making decisions which will affect the galaxy, the universe or the multi-dimensions of creation. We are going to move from being co-heirs to being co-creators – and that is where the fun will really start!

8. The Joshua Generation

We are called as sons to be part of the Joshua Generation, forerunners of heavenly intimacy, who have spied out the land beyond the veil; who have been wooed by the Father into restored sonship. The Joshua Generation are called to experience the precepts, character and nature of God Himself; to experience – and demonstrate – the reality of the very essence of God, who truly is love.

That is what Joshua and Caleb did: they received the inheritance that they knew belonged to them and they helped a whole generation to come into it as well. So the Joshua generation are not just those who do it, they are those who help others to do it too. Joshua and Caleb were two of the twelve spies who were sent ahead into the Promised Land; they saw it was good and they gave a good report (unlike the other ten).

Just because you are in the minority does not mean you are wrong, and we are likely to be in the minority. Joshua and Caleb were in the minority: even amongst the spies they were only two out of twelve; and amongst their own generation of the sons of Israel they were only two out of two and a half million. All the rest died in the wilderness because they did not accept their sonship, seeing themselves as grasshoppers rather than giant-slayers. Joshua and Caleb, it says, had a different spirit.

A generation later, Caleb was 84 years old, still strong and going in and out to war; and he said to Joshua, "Give me the high country." That was Hebron, the best of the land, and there were giants there. So he went and killed them and took possession of what belonged to him. God wants us to be passionate about what belongs to us, not to be disinherited but to inherit the fullness of our inheritance as sons of God.

The Moses generation

So compare that with the Moses generation, because we have all been in the Moses generation (or maybe are still in it). Look at how Moses worked as opposed to how Joshua worked, because they functioned very differently. Moses became a mediator for the people because the people refused to have intimacy with God for themselves, out of fear. They were frightened because they were still slaves in their own minds. They had come out of Egypt but Egypt had not come out of them. They still had a slavery mentality and they brought all their foreign gods out of Egypt and carried them with them into the wilderness (not a good idea). So they ended up with Moses representing them rather than having a relationship with God themselves.

Now the Lord said to Joshua, "This day I will begin to exalt you in the sight of all Israel, so that they will know that just as I have been with Moses, I will be with you. So you shall command the priests who are carrying the ark of the covenant, saying, 'When you come to the edge of the waters of the Jordan, you shall stand still in the Jordan.'" Then Joshua said to the sons of Israel, "Come here, and hear the words of the Lord your God." And Joshua said, "By this you will know that the living God is among you, and that He will assuredly drive out from you the Canaanite, the Hittite, the Hivite, the Perizzite, the Girgashite, the Amorite, and the Jebusite. Behold, the ark of the covenant of the Lord of all the earth is crossing over ahead of you into the Jordan. Now then, take for yourselves twelve men from the tribes of Israel, one man for each tribe. And it will come about when the soles of the feet of the priests who carry the ark of the Lord, the Lord of all the earth, rest in the waters of the Jordan, the waters of the Jordan will be cut off, that is, the waters which are flowing down from above; and they will stand in one heap."

So when the people set out from their tents to cross the Jordan, with the priests carrying the ark of the covenant before the people, and when those who were carrying the ark came up to the Jordan and the feet of the priests carrying the ark stepped down into the edge of the water (for the Jordan overflows all its banks all the days of harvest), then the waters which were flowing down from above stood and rose up in one heap, a great distance away at Adam, the city that is beside Zarethan; and those which were flowing down toward the sea of the Arabah, the Salt Sea, were completely cut off. So the people crossed opposite Jericho (Joshua 3:7-16).

Joshua did things very differently to Moses. Moses parted the Red Sea with his staff. Moses struck the rock and water came out. Moses went into heaven and brought the law and wrote the tablets. Moses did all that for them. When Joshua needed to lead the nation across the Jordan, which was in flood, he brought a heavenly revelation: to take the presence of God in His ark and step into the water, and it would part. Joshua did nothing other than help them hear what God was saying; then the waters parted and they crossed over.

So if Moses had faced Jericho, what would he have done? Probably he would have broken the walls down with his staff. Joshua received heavenly revelation again, and they all marched around it with the presence of God in the ark in their midst, thirteen times in all. Then they all shouted in unison and the walls sank into the earth: they did not collapse and crumple, they actually sank into the earth because the frequency of the vibration of their voices opened the earth beneath the wall.

Now the angel of the presence of God would come into their midst, rather than Moses going up the mountain for a private audience. So everything was done differently. Everything had changed. This is why understanding 'the new versus the old' is important. The transition out of the wilderness into the Promised Land is quite difficult when you are used to doing things in an old way and God suddenly starts to give you new ways of doing things. We have to make sure that we do not revert to old covenant 'Moses' ways in the new covenant.

In a Moses generation, a mediator represents the people before God, tells the people what God has said and generally does everything for them. We are full of that in the church today: priestly, earthly coverings. In the new covenant there is no earthly priesthood. Yes, we are all kings and priests but we are not supposed to be kings and priests on the earth, we are supposed to be kings and priests in heaven. On earth we are supposed to be oracles and legislators (or prophets and apostles) because those are the foundations of what we do on earth; in heaven we are a royal priesthood. Unfortunately we have gone back to old covenant models of earthly priests, an Aaronic order of priests, in which they get to do the intimate things with God and the rest of us do not. That is a perversion; that is an old covenant not new covenant perspective.

The Moses generation generally has a top-down hierarchical governmental structure. Someone is at the top, whether it be the apostle or the prophet or the pastor or the leadership team or whatever you call them, there will always be someone who is on top and everyone else ultimately has to fall in line with what they say.

The Moses generation resists change. They resist change because it means giving up their positions of authority, and for some of them, giving up their livelihood and the ministries and businesses they have built in the kingdom. Now God is telling them to cross over and stop telling people what to do, or cross over and stop giving them prophetic words but start teaching them to hear God for themselves.

I used to go to a lot of prophetic conferences. Why? Because I wanted to get a word from God. But I expected it to come through the prophet; God was speaking to me during those times but I was not listening to Him because I wanted the word from the prophet, the professional who knew how to hear God. I never got one. In fact, the same people seemed to get them every time. In the end I got frustrated and stopped going, because what was the point of spending time and money to go when I was not getting anything? That was all part of my journey. God wanted to speak to me Himself, I was just not able to hear very clearly; and if I had got accustomed

99

to Him speaking to me through someone else, I would never have really engaged to hear Him for myself.

I am not saying that there is no place for ministries that are called prophetic or apostolic. I do believe fivefold ministry still exists: it is an earthly ministry to help equip us here (on earth) to engage there (in heaven). It is not to engage there for us. I do not believe in earthly rabbis, earthly priests, or earthly ministers. We are all ministers and we are all under one rabbi: He is called Jesus. He wants to teach us in relationship, and we can all hear His voice.

So there is resistance. Some people are afraid to let go of the old because their whole livelihood is caught up with it; and some people I know are being called by God to leave where they are and move into the Promised Land but they are not going. And I do not want them to die in the wilderness.

We were never supposed to build in the wilderness. The Israelites built nothing there, they travelled lightly and they were able to break camp whenever God said to move. But some people have built ministries in the wilderness; they have mountains of their authority in the wilderness; and God is saying "Leave all this and cross over." If they had never built there in the first place, there would not be so much to let go of. Some of them are the very ministries that talk about an open heaven and engaging heaven, yet they are not facilitating people doing it themselves, they are resisting it. What is worse, not only are they not going themselves, but they are actively stopping other people from going who are hearing the call of God, and they are putting hindrances in the way of those people engaging in heaven for themselves.

The Moses generation lacks true sonship identity. They generally have a fear of man and often a one-man-ministry focus. The Joshua generation are those who embrace their inheritance, their birthright as sons of God, and live in the freedom of the relationship of an open heaven and open veil. We cannot be sons in the Joshua generation without a relationship with our Father and we cannot have a relationship with our Father without a relationship with Jesus. He is the Way, the Truth and the Life. He is the door: no one can come to the Father but through Jesus – that is absolutely non-negotiable for me – but the Holy Spirit does not just do it in one or two different ways; there are many ways He can bring people to the Father through Jesus, and some of them may appear unexpected if you have a religious mindset.

From slavery to sonship

A relationship with our Father releases us from slavery and brings us into sonship. We are no longer slaves, or servants, or stewards. That does not mean that we do not desire to serve the purposes of God, but we do not do it as slaves, we do it as sons.

There is a process to go through. We may call it a number of different names – such as transfiguration, or transformation, or metamorphosis – but essentially they all mean 'change'. Sonship means change: you cannot stay a slave and expect to operate as a son. Our mind needs to be renewed: that means our soul needs to be restored and made whole, and our physical body needs to come back into complete health and wholeness (because we do need a body to operate here on earth: if you do not have a body on earth you are going to be stuck in heaven, or perhaps showing up sometimes in the spiritual realm, but you will not have the authority that a person who has a physical body has on earth). We need to be matured in body, soul and spirit.

Sonship brings the responsibility to rule and bring dominion. That was God's original call to Adam and Eve: to be fruitful, to multiply, to fill the earth, to subdue and to rule. That was never to rule over each other, it was to rule over the environment, to make it habitable and blessed so that everyone could prosper and increase. But of course we tried to rule over each other, which led to the formation of all the nations of the world and all the conflict that ensues. All because we are trying to make a name for ourselves rather than to honour God's name.

101

That was why the Tower of Babel happened, as described in Genesis 11. "Let's make a name for ourselves; otherwise we will be scattered abroad over the face of all the earth." Well, what they feared came upon them, and they were indeed scattered all over the earth; but they still made names for themselves, and they called them nations. We are still suffering from nations competing with one another, whereas God told Abram to bring blessing to every family of the earth. There is a huge difference between family and nations: when we discover how to rule as God intends, it will involve restoration of family.

The Joshua generation

The Joshua generation are sons who have been through the wilderness years of preparation. I had years of going through the wilderness, going round and round the mountain so many times that I got to the point where I had had enough. It was desperation, I think. My spirit was calling out on God, "There must be more than this!" That song by U2 was my theme song, "I Still Haven't Found What I'm Looking For." It was true. I had not found it, though I had been searching for it my whole life. Now I have found it: being at home with the Father in heaven and being a gateway from heaven into the earth.

The Joshua generation are those who are spying out the Promised Land beyond the veil. Now some of us are having our first experiences of that, maybe just a few 'forerunners of forerunners' for now, but if you are still reading this, then you too are a forerunner, because the vast majority of the Christian community would have no idea what I am talking about at all – they sometimes tell me so in their YouTube comments – but they will, because God is calling them. And beyond that, there is also a whole world of people out there who do not yet know God, and they are going to be the 'next generation.'

That is not just young people: it will include young people but it will be people of all ages. The problem when this call to reach a harvest first went out in 1975 was that churches and ministries began to try to reap their own harvest of young people; they spent all their money and effort on trying to do youth work or young people's ministry. There was some success with it, but what they did not do was raise up the mentors for when those young people would come. Most of those young people therefore did not have the Joshua generation to enable them to come into their full inheritance, so they just got what their parents had got... and that is why they still got stuck in the wilderness.

Let us hear and respond to the call to enter beyond the veil and take up our royal positions in heaven. That is where the real royal priesthood functions, seated in heavenly places as priests and kings of God. Let us be willing to mentor the next generation of the harvest.

Now I believe that this next harvest is going to be the harvest of the harvesters, so prophetically it is a billion people, which means there are many of them still to come. After that, like Joshua and Caleb, let us say to the next generation, "Cross over and receive your inheritance." We are going to walk with them in that inheritance: I am not passing the baton to anybody, I am going to walk together with them so that together we can function as sons of God. Not us as fathers and them as sons; we should have the characteristics of fatherhood but without making ourselves out to be fathers to other people, because God is their Father.

We are all His sons, walking together in relationship with our Father. I am not going to be anyone's earthly father because then they will be looking to me rather than looking to God. I am a son coming alongside them: I may know a little more, have a little more experience, and I am going to pass that on. I am not going to hold it to myself. Knowledge can be power: and some people are not passing on what they know to others because if they keep it to themselves they can maintain their positions of power. Freely we have received; freely we give. It is not without value – it has a real value – but we give it because we have received it. Therefore we do need to receive it.

We need to help and equip people to receive their heavenly, supernatural inheritance so that they too are seated in heavenly places. It is not that all of us who are of the Joshua generation are going to be seated on the thrones of heaven and be over all those who are on the earth. No, we are all going to be in heaven: we are all seated in heavenly places and we need to help equip everyone else to be there and engage with that reality.

Are we willing to establish storehouses on earth, or embassies of heaven on earth, or *ekklesias* on earth that are ready for that harvest? That is what the Joshua generation are about, preparing for a harvest. Now I hear some mystics talking about having experiences but I do not hear too many of them talking about a harvest, because they seem to be very focused on all the heavenly experiences without realising that it all has to be outworked on earth. There has to be an earthly outworking: we have to earth it out.

What is the point of doing amazing things in heaven if it makes no earthly difference? That is why we have set up a ministry to help people here in our town who are suffering from poverty, homelessness and addiction, because that is the mandate we have been given. Other people have other mandates, but if we all want to transform our communities we have to see heaven change earth. We have to see heaven manifested on earth so that earth becomes like heaven. We are not going to get that if we are just having a great time in heaven and never outworking anything here. When there is an outworking into the earth to bring transformation, creation itself will respond to that.

Let us be ready for that harvest. I believe that God's plan is for three generations to work in unity together to establish God's government. His government always works in threes: Father, Son and Spirit. That is why we have benches of three who are foundational government on the earth. We need to see three generations come together: it has never happened since Abraham, Isaac and Jacob (remember that God identified Himself as 'the God of Abraham, Isaac and Jacob',

104

and there was a governmental aspect to that). Moses and Joshua could have been the next step, but the Moses generation refused to go in, so Joshua had to go and start again.

The Joshua generation needs to rise up and be ready for the next generation, to be ready for those supernatural harvesters so that two generations reach out to the third. Those three generations, if we can get them working together, can be instrumental in seeing the kingdom of God outworked on earth and throughout creation in ways which are beyond our comprehension today. I really do not want to miss it, and I intend to be around for it!

Now these things happened to them as an example, and they were written for our instruction, upon whom the ends of the ages have come (1 Corinthians 10:11).

As the Joshua generation, we have to learn the lessons of the previous generation and not make the same mistakes. God showed them their inheritance in the Promised Land yet they refused to go in, so they continued living in the wilderness. The wilderness was a miraculous place: their clothes did not wear out and they were provided with food every day from heaven. Despite their grumbling and complaining, God still blessed them.

To go into the Promised Land they would have to step out of their accustomed place of immaturity where God did it all for them. Now they would have to go in and take possession. And God did not drive the other nations out in front of them, He just prepared the Israelites to be able to drive them out. The inhabitants of the land were frightened of the children of Israel; but the majority of the children of Israel were frightened of the inhabitants of the land, so they did not go in. But Joshua and Caleb were different.

So Moses did things one way; Joshua did things in a different way. God has been calling out of heaven, releasing a sound (a vibrational frequency) that carries this message, and it has

105

been connecting with people's spirits. The reason you picked up this book is likely because something has drawn you to realise that you are not satisfied with the wilderness anymore; you want something of the promises that belong to you as a son. That sense of eternity in your heart has been connecting you with that desire and you want more. The spirits of God's children are resonating with that sound. There is something creating this agreement that is drawing us into our inheritance, crying out "There must be more than this!"

Wake up!

Over forty years ago, a prophet called Bob Jones released this sound in heaven. It was on 8/8/1975, and it was a prophecy of a billion soul harvest; a call to raise up a Joshua generation of supernatural mentors; a call to spy out our supernatural inheritance beyond the veil. The church missed the call. They raised up evangelists and youth workers and tried to reap a harvest.

But the call was really, "Hey, heaven's open!" Bob Jones used to talk all the time about being in heaven and engaging the angels; but he did not equip others to do it, he kept it a mystery. That is part of the reason people did not embrace the call: there were mysteries attached to it that were never released, no one was equipped to go and engage in heaven, and therefore there was only an earthly outworking. We need to avoid making that same mistake.

Over the forty years from 1975 to 2015, we saw a huge increase in the activity of the Holy Spirit and in dreams, visions and ecstatic encounters. God was going to break through, whether those people were going to release that revelation or not. He almost circumvented that whole movement and reached people in spite of it.

So, sons, arise! We need to wake up and arise from our sleep. That is really what God has been saying for the last 40 years: "You can hear Me! You can come into heaven! Why are you going to prophetic conferences? Why are you asking the apostle for a vision? Come to Me!"

Or, as Morpheus put it in the *Matrix* movie, "Wake up, Neo, the Matrix has you!" We have been living under an illusion, a delusion. A veil of religion has been pulled over our eyes and we have not been able to see the truth of who we are. That is changing. We need to arise and shine as stars, restored to our positions of heavenly government.

In 2012 I prophesied the beginning of a three-year period of preparation. As a local church we then went through a really difficult three years (which included that four months of preparation for me) culminating on 8/8/2015, forty years to the day after Bob Jones' prophecy. That eighth month had three days which were eight-eight-eight, which is symbolic of new beginnings: 8th, 17th [1+7=8] and 26th [2+6=8]) - and the year, 2015 (2+0+1+5=8).

So August 2015 was the end of what was figuratively a Moses generation – and it ushered in a new governmental order of new beginnings. That was when people started talking about the order of Melchizedek, and the heavenly priesthood rather than the earthly priesthood; the Joshua generation, living according to the order of Melchizedek, engaging with the four faces of God, engaging in the name of God.

Arthur Burke (whose scientific method appeals to me because he is very empirical in his research and evidence-based conclusions) prophesied the end of the ruler and the beginning of the priests. I am not sure what interpretation he himself put on his prophecy, but I certainly responded to it. I believe it marked a call for deep to call to deep.

Back in 2012, someone sent me a book called *When Heaven Touches Earth* (co-authored by Mark Virkler, who I very much respect as someone who helps people to hear the voice of God). The message behind it was a call for the reformation of church, to restore angelic and heavenly encounters as the norm rather than an exception. He asked 95 leaders around the world to sign it and endorse it, like Luther pinned his 95 theses on the church door. So I read it, and I thought it was at least a start! This was after I had been in heaven and had many heavenly experiences, so for me this was just normal, everyday life. But people from right across a whole spectrum of different streams endorsed this book, and I believe that it was an indication of the beginning of the end of the old, foreshadowing a new beginning.

August 2015 was a turning point. Sometimes there are *kairos* moments in time, in which God does something significant, and this was one of them. It had been building for some time. I have talked to lots of people who had engagements in 2010: there were awakenings during which people started to get an opening in their hearts. In 2012 Ian Clayton began talking about the end of the fivefold ministry order of government, the apostolic order, which he aligned with the Mayan calendar ending on 20th of December 2012 (and that was actually the end of one complete cycle of the circle of the deep, the constellations, which is something very significant.). I think it was indeed the end of their government, but not of their function, because they retain an earthly function.

This began the reformation of the church into the *ekklesia* of God. I hesitate to use the English word 'church' now to describe what God is doing because people hear that word and have a well-established traditional understanding of what it means. The word *'ekklesia'* carries a different connotation. An *ekklesia* comprises people gathered around a blueprint of dominion from a heavenly position into the earth. And God is releasing blueprints to people around the world to form benches of three around that blueprint to begin to establish heaven on earth.

And there we were in 2015, 8-8-8, a time of triple new beginnings. It was a really interesting time, the end of the old generation and the beginning of the new. Now God is taking the kingdom from those who are operating in the wilderness, and giving it to those who are operating in heaven.

"Therefore I say to you, the kingdom of God will be taken away from you and given to a people producing its fruit" (Mathew 21:43).

Jesus was talking there about the old and the new covenant. Those in the wilderness are not producing the full fruit and therefore the authority is moving away from them. Some of the major figures leading those ministries and groups, well-known people in the old order, are even dying physically without having responded to the call to cross over. But, as I have said many times before, God would rather have an amateur in the new than an expert in the old, and that qualifies all of us to embrace the call of God to receive a blueprint out of heaven and see it outworked on the earth.

So I believe that kingdom government has been removed from the old order. Now, as the order of Melchizedek, as the Joshua generation, we can embrace being seated in heavenly places, and crossing over into our inheritance in heaven to outwork that on the earth. As you read this, I want you to hear the call. Get your spirit to listen to the call that is calling you to rise up as that Joshua generation and take your place, seated in the heavenly realms; and be willing to receive blueprints from heaven to establish things on the earth. That is ultimately what God wants: heaven manifested on earth. It is not enough to be heavenly tourists, taking trips into heaven. It is great to explore and have fun but there is a more serious purpose to it as well, and that is to see heavenly government manifested here on the earth.

9. A Good Report

The Joshua generation have a different spirit and will be willing to face the obstacles.

The Joshua generation are giant-slayers.

The Joshua generation will enable the next generation to engage their full supernatural heavenly inheritance.

The Joshua generation will also be the Joseph, Daniel and Enoch generation.

Joshua, Joseph, Daniel and Enoch

At a conference a few years ago, I was engaged in worship when those four came and stood next to me. It was a very intense experience: I very strongly engaged with them, and they held up my hands. I got a sense that they were helping me to realise that the Joshua generation has input from others. We call it the Joshua generation, but you could equally well call it the Joseph generation, the Daniel generation or the Enoch generation, because the characteristics of those four particularly (though there are probably others too) are key for us.

Enoch

Enoch walked with God in heaven and on earth. He was known as the 'star walker'; he had access to the realms of heaven, and one day He did not come back. When I first met him in heaven, he told me I should read *The Book of Enoch* – he did not write it, but it is a book which expresses his life and the various things he saw. So I thought I had better read it, or I would be really embarrassed the next time I saw him. It was heavy going but it had prophetic insight: insight into the days before the flood and insight into his relationship with God and what he was saying in terms of our day.

So Enoch is a good example for us that when we walk with God we have access to another realm. You can engage with

Enoch in the realms of heaven, as I have; and as I said earlier, he gave me a lot of quests. He assigned me things to do, and because he didn't die physically he still has an investment into our day which goes beyond some of the cloud of witnesses. He is not exactly one of them, because he is someone who was taken into that realm (the same is true of Elijah).

Daniel

Daniel, as we know, was a prophet who had a number of apocalyptic-type experiences and was able to describe them.

"But as for you, Daniel, conceal these words and seal up the book until the end of time; many will go back and forth, and knowledge will increase" (Daniel 12:4).

This is primarily talking about the state of the world at the time of the Roman Empire, which saw a great increase in movement and knowledge; but Daniel's intention in coming to stand beside me was to encourage and support me. So I think there is also an application of this to the present day, when we are able to share information instantly, people travel all over the world, and journeys that used to take weeks and months can now be done in hours.

And if we are learning to transrelocate in the spirit, then that too can be instant: we are not limited by space and time so we can translate in the spirit and transrelocate physically. A number of times I have transrelocated physically and been in another place instantly; at other times I have translated into another realm in the spirit. And when people have engaged me in that realm or in that place, it was as if my spirit just appeared to them like my physical form: they were able to touch me and I was able to touch them, but I knew it was my spirit because I was aware that I was still physically somewhere else.

All those things are happening in our days, and you have plenty of other people besides me talking about that kind of experience, such as Bruce Allen, Michael Van Vlymen and of course Ian Clayton. So it is not just that many are going back and forth in a technological sense, it is also happening in the supernatural.

I believe that Daniel was showing me that the revelation he received was sealed up for the new covenant age and is available for us today. Throughout the new covenant age mystics have engaged that revelation because the books are now open. The revelation we are getting concerning the realms of heaven and how to engage God in those realms is because we have discovered that truth in our generation. In that case, let us be sure to embrace it.

Joseph

I love the story of Joseph because it is the story of his preparation for destiny. He saw his destiny in his dreams: that he would be such a person in government that even his family would bow down to him. But he was rather immature and brash about it, so he had to go through a process of transformation in which he would learn to trust God in even the most difficult of circumstances.

His life was a series of injustices. Injustice is very difficult to face because it is not fair. "You've given me these dreams and now they've thrown me in a pit and sent me off to Egypt, and I was serving in this house and now he's accused me, and his wife's accused me, and here I am in prison, and all I did was take what you said and believe it!" Sometimes our life takes us on quite a strange journey to get us to a place where eventually we can fulfil what God is calling us to do.

Joseph was in the dungeon, which does not seem like a particularly good place to start. But events can happen and circumstances change very quickly when you are able to respond to your destiny. Pharaoh sent and called for Joseph, so they hurriedly brought him out of the dungeon, having shaved and changed his clothes. So everything changed for him. Why? Because he was able to hear the voice of God and share that with insight and revelation. And then (see Genesis 41:38) Pharaoh said to his servants, "Can we find a man like this, in whom is a divine spirit?" Well, this book is for people like that, for people like you, who have the divine spirit. You have the capacity to come out of obscurity and right into the centre of the world stage. Joseph was thrust from prison to become the second-in-command in the whole of Egypt, with insight and wisdom of what to do. Even Pharaoh knew it was God:

So Pharaoh said to Joseph, "Since God has informed you of all this, there is no one as discerning and wise as you are. You shall be over my house, and according to your command all my people shall do homage; only in the throne I will be greater than you" (Genesis 41:39-40).

It is important for us to hear the voice of God so that we know what to do in certain times and seasons, just as the sons of Issachar did (see 1 Chronicles 12:32). Joseph had maintained his relationship with God through all the apparent injustices he suffered, and God was now fulfilling his destiny. It took a long time, and sometimes we can get weary and worn out with trying to do what God said, and the visions and the dreams we have. But God knows the time that we are called for, so when Esther shows up and says "You are called for a time such as this," I take notice. And that is becoming a fulfilment of our destiny in which we may come from obscurity and be placed into a totally different realm of government, as happened for Joseph.

Pharaoh elevated him to second in the kingdom, a place of considerable power and authority. Joseph was clearly not Egyptian, but his race did not matter, his background did not matter: when God put him into that place, there he was. We see that God engineered the situation, but Joseph responded; and then he outworked his wisdom:

So he gathered all the food of these seven years which occurred in the land of Egypt and placed the food in the cities; he placed in every city the food from its own surrounding fields... The people of all the earth came to Egypt to buy grain from Joseph, because the famine was severe in all the earth (Genesis 41:48, 57).

113

Then the whole world came to him. I believe that when we begin to establish the cities of refuge, *ekklesias* and embassies of heaven, the world will come. The 'church' may not come, but the world will, because they will recognise the true nature of the sons of God. Joseph gathered 20% of the food and stored it up. I believe prophetically that is a picture of the 20% of the world harvest, the billion people harvest, who need to come into the storehouses. Then the world will be ready to receive them and embrace them in their supernatural role as harvesters, labourers for the harvest fields about which Jesus said that they are white unto harvest but the labourers are few (see Luke 10:2). They have been few throughout history, but I believe that now, as we embrace our call to help raise them up, that God is going to release a harvest – but it will only come about if we have the storehouses ready.

I see in Joseph a picture of what can be for every one of our lives: quickly and supernaturally to be put in place to fulfil our destiny, whatever has gone before. Joseph came out of the prison and out of obscurity to administer a nation and set up storehouses for the harvest, and then the whole world – including his brothers who had originally rejected him – eventually came to him. So there is still hope for those of the church who are not embracing what God is doing: God has not given up on them. He is continuing to call them, and maybe some of what they see in us may turn their hearts to cross over to the Promised Land themselves.

A good report

So the question is, are we prepared to be forerunners? Are we even 'prepared to be prepared'? God will have to prepare us so that we are ready. That is a challenge. It requires a change, a transformation. Are we ready to cross over and give a good report to others of what we have experienced? That is what Joshua and Caleb did: "This is what God has said: we can take this. This is ours – it belongs to us!"

When we have experiences in the realms of heaven, with the angelic realm and in the supernatural dimension, we will have

114

to find a way of communicating those experiences that does not alienate people, a way they can receive them. Sometimes that means we do not dump everything on people all at once, because it might be difficult to take in all that I am sharing with you here (perhaps you are even finding it difficult yourself – if there is anything that does not resonate with you, park it, ask God about it, come back to it when you are ready). So we might give them a little at a time, to get their attention and open up their hearts so that they can receive more and become hungry for the things we share testimony of. But let us be wise in how we present it, because we can share it in a way that sounds elitist, as if we think we have got it all right and they have got it all wrong. We have to be very careful that we do not think or operate in that way. Yet we also have to believe in what we have experienced enough not to hide it or be reticent about where we are going on our journey, because that will help other people come along too.

Are we willing to operate as sons of God in the realms of heaven? Are we willing to be servant-hearted leaders who will promote the next generation? Yes, leaders. Maybe you do not want to be a leader? Maybe that seems like too much responsibility? All right, but whether you like it or not, you have a role in the kingdom as a son of God. Whether you want it or not, you have been called for a time such as this, to embrace the government of God as a son. That will be outworked for different people in many different ways, but in the end it comes down to "am I willing to serve?" That is the message: Jesus came to serve and not be served. So in everything that God is doing in this generation He is raising up, we will have a humble heart to serve others; we are not here to rule over people (as the Moses generation did – or are still doing).

Free access

There is a process that will bring us to this maturity of government and it requires our cooperation: to embrace the refiner's fire of transformation. All of us have to embrace the

115

fire. We can choose when, but eventually we will have to, so let us be proactive and embrace it now. That process is relational and flows from the place of rest. When we know God's love it is easier to embrace His fire because we know His fire is His love. If we have doubts about God's love, and maybe a little bit of fear, then sometimes we might shy away from being on that altar and from embracing it.

"Thus says the LORD of hosts, 'If you will walk in My ways and if you will perform My service, then you will also govern My house and also have charge of My courts, and I will grant you free access among these who are standing here'" (Zechariah 3:7).

The process entails us being humble and faithful in the little that we have been given, and then we will start to receive more. This scripture is a description of that process. Joshua the high priest was in heaven, in the court of heaven, and had just been clothed in robes of righteousness and given his position in the favour of God's blessing as His son.

"If you will walk in My ways": that is what we do here on the earth. We walk in His ways day by day, expressing the nature of God's love in our daily lives.

"If you will perform My service" – in other words, if you will start outworking His government – "then you will govern My house". His house, first of all, is each of us, because we are the house of God; and then it is the mountain of the house of the Lord – and that might be a local expression, a regional expression or beyond.

"And also have charge of My courts": not just have access to the courts, but have charge of them. "And I will grant you free access among these who are standing here" (they were standing in the assembly of God).

All this becomes available to us if we are willing to accept our position of sonship as a forerunner in the Joshua generation. Then we have access to the different courts in heaven and to the different realms of heaven: all that becomes open to us when we are in our position seated in the heavenly places.

If we are not seated in the heavenly places and are not willing to embrace our destiny and our call, then we can generally access the mobile court and not much else; but when we step into that realm, are seated in that realm and are progressively elevated into different roles then we get access to all those places.

So we need to know our identity as sons of God first and foremost. Identity releases position. It will release our position as a friend of God, a lord, king, priest, oracle, legislator, scribe, magistrate, judge, chancellor. We are given a heavenly position as well as an earthly position. Our earthly position is always going to be in the foundations because we are all called here to demonstrate humility and serve. There, we may be given different roles of government but it is still to serve. It is all about serving – blessing, empowering, releasing, encouraging – because that is what God wants to do with us. It is our position there that releases our authority to establish the kingdom in heaven and be a gateway into the earth.

As we get the revelation of this, what we used to do before stops working. So if you have been an intercessor, you will find that intercession does not work anymore because God does not want you to intercede here, trying to get through some atmosphere to reach Him, He wants to take you above the atmosphere so that you have direct access to Him, heart to heart. Then you can intercede, which we do in the courts of heaven in a totally different way. And that is just one example. If things that we have been used to doing do not work anymore, it is because God wants to show us that there is a higher, more effective, more powerful way.

Dawning of a new day

I was in a state of intimacy with God, and He said this. "My children are sons of man – not the first man, Adam, but the last man, Jesus. You are also sons of God, co-heirs and co-creators, full representations of My image and My government, seated in the heavens and walking on the earth. Son, do you feel it? Do you sense it? Do you hear it? Can you see it? The dawning of a new day, the beginning of a new season: a new vista, a new horizon." And I could, because I was in a state where the revelation of what He was trying to impart to me was open.

Things are beginning to be unveiled. Some people are beginning to sense it and it is drawing them. Some people may see it, some may sense it or feel it or just hear the sound: something is changing, something is happening. We are coming out of obscurity into positions of authority – in heaven to start with, but that may also outwork on the earth as we establish heaven on the earth in embassies of heaven and *ekklesias*.

"Can you not hear? Can you not see?" (And some people really cannot). "Then feel the wind shift, feel its intensity increase. Because it is happening: just be open to it in different ways. I call My sons to arise and take their places so that you can see, hear, perceive and know that the ordinances of heaven have been decreed and the legions of heaven are being prepared to engage the atmosphere of the earth."

Very few places that I have ever visited or seen have dealt with the atmosphere of the earth in their sphere of responsibility. We are going to have to deal with it if we are going to get the everlasting doors open over us. It will have to be cleared and occupied by the legitimate angelic rulers, principalities and powers that God has assigned. Are we ready for that?

We are not going to engage in some kind of pseudo-military mission of spiritual warfare, battling against principalities and powers. If you do that you are going to run into trouble. That is not our role. Our role is to work with, cooperate with and assign those whose role it is to go and take those places, but we will need to use the courts of heaven to deal with the legal rights that the usurpers have to be there. Therefore we really need to start to learn how to legislate, to govern and to rule.

I have seen (and taken part in) a lot of what was termed 'spiritual warfare', which hardly ever worked. People just got worn out from screaming at the heavens and shouting, binding this and pulling down that. Unless God gave you a very specific mandate to do it, it was never very successful, and a lot of people became damaged and disappointed by it.

"This will only be in cooperation with those who have established a beachhead of heaven on the earth, with heaven's blueprints and heaven's government demonstrated."

This is for those who are ready to take their places and receive that revelation and cooperate. We have to have something on earth to show for all this. It is great to go exploring the heavens – great that we have some fantastic explorers out there who are saying "Hey, there are amazing things over here for you!" – but someone has to go and take possession of it all and bring it onto the earth. Explorers are not necessarily the best people to do that: we need pioneers who will take the ground and then occupy it. We have to establish heaven on the earth. So we need *ekklesias* that are operating according to this new order; we need embassies of heaven; we need people who will be willing to get a blueprint and establish a foundation.

You do not need hundreds of people to start with. In fact, if you have hundreds of people trying to do it you are going to run into a lot of difficulties. I would suggest we do this from scratch: get three people who can establish a bench of three, or ten people who can be established as a bench of three and a bench of seven. You only need a handful of people who can get the foundations relationally in place, strong and deep, so that when these things start to happen, God will add to that overnight. Groups of ten can be a hundred overnight, and a thousand over another night, because we will be ready to receive the harvest, we will be ready to disciple and equip and release those who are coming. But we have got to be ready, so we will need to be equipped. We need to know how to do these things ourselves and to know how to share that with others. I believe we are in a time in which we are being prepared in heaven, but we need also to start to prepare here.

Change is coming. You can be part of it; you can miss it; you can even resist it; you cannot stop it. Gathering angels are going to be released to bring in the firstfruits of the harvest to those who are prepared, where the atmosphere is cleansed and the government is in place.

Do not think, "Oh, let's go and do that right now!" No. We have to be in the position of authority to be able to do it, so we have to mature and take our places in heaven so that we can learn how to govern, learn how to rule. It is not going to happen for us all tomorrow, but it is going to start happening for those who have prepared and have got ready. So I want to encourage you to start believing for something more.

Remember, Joshua and Caleb were in their 80s when they started this; they were still strong, and Joshua went on until he was 120 years old. Our age is irrelevant. We do not have to be a young person in that sense: we can be young in heart and young in mind, and then we can be young in body to be able to do everything that God has called us to do. We will never run out of time to fulfil our destiny. God gives us the ability to be able to fulfil everything He has called us to do, but we have to cooperate with Him and 'get with the program' of being transformed into sons.

Activation #8: The Council of the Upright

Those four men in white linen who came to engage with me were those who were assigned to help me engage with the Joshua generation, to call it and to equip it and do what I am doing. There are other men in white linen who have been assigned to us as a ministry: twelve of them, who are there as a council for us, and they are invested in what we do. We can all have some of those witnesses assigned to our lives. Just as God has assigned angels, He is also assigning members of the cloud of witnesses who are surrounding us, looking on and wanting to be involved.

We can engage the Council of the Upright for the Joshua generation and for our lives. We will take some time now to do that. Has God assigned someone to you to help you? When you connect with that person (or those people) it will begin to stir you in your destiny.

I do not know who you are going to engage with, but I suggest you ask Jesus or the Father to introduce you to them. When you meet them, do ask them why they are connected to you; get to know them, and receive the wisdom and insight that they may have for you.

Now you might be thinking, "Surely I can just go to God and He will tell me all that kind of thing?" We need to understand that He has assigned others to have particular roles in heaven. For example, there are people in heaven writing dreams for those still on earth, dreams that are introducing them to the supernatural dimensions of God. The cloud of witnesses are not all up there sitting on a cloud with harps, making sweet melody: they have roles to play in the kingdom. They are part of the Church of the Firstborn who are enrolled in heaven, and we are part of the Church of the Firstborn who are still on earth, so let us be open to engage them.

As usual, you can read and follow the guided engagement here or listen to the audio version either from the resources page online or by scanning the QR code.

Ask Jesus or ask the Father to introduce those who are assigned to you. If you have never engaged like this, just go with it and be open to whatever happens: whatever you sense or receive, just trust that God is in it and be prepared to follow it through.

> We have an open heaven.
> Jacob's ladder is here for us,
> and we can walk up those steps into heaven.

> As you close your eyes,
> begin to think of that ladder going from earth to heaven.
> Think about those steps,

and that there is a door open
and that you have an invitation to "Come up here."

Picture that open door in your mind.
Go up those steps and cross over through the veil.
Enter into the realm of the kingdom.

Jesus is always waiting for us in that open door.
We can present ourselves to Him as our high priest,
as a living sacrifice,
and say whatever we want to Him.

First, hear the call to be part of the Joshua generation.
Let your spirit respond to the call.

(It is the same call that I have released to you before, but
I want you to hear it from heaven, not just from the earth.)

So in the realms of heaven,
in the atmosphere of heaven,
as you stand with Jesus in that realm,
hear the Father calling:

"Son I call your spirit to attention.
Spirit, listen as a true son.

"I call forth your identity as part of the Joshua generation,
a son of the order of Melchizedek.

"I call forth your destiny to manifest God's kingdom
on earth as it is in heaven.

"I call forth your destiny to fill the earth with God's glory.

"I call forth your identity, destiny and authority as lords
to administrate God's rule on earth as it is in heaven.

"I call forth your identity, destiny and authority as kings
to have charge over the heavenly courts.

"I call forth your identity, destiny and authority as sons
to stand in God's presence and be displayed on the earth.

"I call forth your identity, destiny and authority as sons of
God to answer the groan of creation,
to restore it to its original condition and purpose.

"I call forth the Joshua generation to rise up
and take possession of their inheritance."

Let those words resonate with you.
Let your spirit jump and leap at the call.
Respond to it with a "yes."

Hear "You are my beloved Son in whom I am well pleased."
Receive God's affirmation, acceptance, approval and
recognition,
everything that He wants to express to you
to validate Himself to you as your Father,
and you as His son.

And now I want to encourage you to ask Jesus to take
you to the Court of the Upright.

Ask Him to take you by the hand,
take you through the veils,
and take you through the door into that court.

Ask Him to introduce any of the cloud of witnesses that
are assigned to your life,
assigned to your destiny,
assigned to your ministry.

Let Him introduce you
to the council that may be prepared for you,
or any individuals who have an investment in your life.

Just embrace that,
and allow the presence of God to lead you into that
engagement.
Be open to receive and embrace it.

Stay in that place as long as you wish.

Now this is just an introduction, the beginning of something which you will need to continue to engage for yourself and then follow through. We need all the help we can get. The men in white linen have access to revelation that they want to release to us, and so they help us.

If you were not able to engage with them this time, or you are not sure, then set the desire of your heart upon engaging them and they will seek you out. I can look into the realm of the spirit and see when they start observing us: there is activity and excitement because it is their strong desire to engage with us and help us.

10. Fire Stones

"You were in Eden, the garden of God;
Every precious stone was your covering:
The ruby, the topaz and the diamond;
The beryl, the onyx and the jasper;
The lapis lazuli, the turquoise and the emerald;
And the gold, the workmanship of your settings and sockets,
Was in you.
On the day that you were created
They were prepared.

"You were the anointed cherub who covers,
And I placed you there.
You were on the holy mountain of God;
You walked in the midst of the stones of fire" (Ezekiel 28:13-
14).

This passage is usually taken to be referring to Lucifer, before
he rebelled. What he was covering was the Ark (or Arc) of
God's Presence, so he was looking into the very deep things
of God. He was on the holy mountain of God, which is where
the garden is, and he walked in the midst of the stones of fire.

On his body he had nine stones that were supposed to release
the light of the revelation that he was covering to the sons of
man. Those stones on his body have a connection to the fire
stones amongst which he walked. We were to receive that
revelation from him and to mature. So if Lucifer had not
rebelled, and if Adam had not fallen, mankind would have
received that intended revelation and been able to grow into
maturity. But now, as God's sons, we have access to engage
the fire stones directly.

My first encounter

Engagements with the fire stones of destiny have been very
significant encounters on my journey. My first encounter with
them was my very first engagement in heaven, back in 2008,
which as I have described earlier, was completely involuntary.

I was in the Freedom Centre, sitting in my office, preparing for a prophetic workshop. We were in the midst of a time when God was pouring out His Spirit: people were having dreams and visions, and other supernatural manifestations were going on. I stayed after everyone had gone home and I was just at my desk, meditating and asking God if there was anything He wanted to say or do.

All of a sudden a portal opened up in the desk and I was sucked right through it and found myself in heaven (though at first I had no idea where I was). I was beside a river of fire, which was my first clue. I knew that in Daniel it says that there is a river of fire coming from the throne of God, so I started to think, "Okay, the river of fire is here, so how do I get to the throne of God?"

I set my heart on it and asked God "How do I get there?" He showed me the fire stones. Again, I had no idea that was what I was seeing, they just looked like a swirling mass of quantum energy. That is the only way I can describe it. It was like looking into their subatomic structure and seeing the life that was in them. The colour was just amazing. They were arranged like steps going upwards, and I thought, "Wow! So I guess I can walk up these steps."

I stepped onto the first one and I was totally transfixed. I had stepped into a level of love that I had never experienced before. It was the first fruit of the Spirit, the very nature of God as love, and as I stood on the step it was as if I became part of it. I became love. It was deeply emotional. I would have said I was not generally an emotional person, but I was totally immersed in this experience and I just stayed there, not wanting to move, being cocooned in this love. It was going deeper than mere emotion: I felt the life and the energy that was in it and it stirred up passion in my heart.

After some time I managed to move, because, after all, I wanted to get to the throne of God. I took another step and it was joy. It was not the joy of laughter, it was the joy that Jesus said that we would have to make our joy full, a deep, deep sense of joy.

I stepped on every stone: love, joy, peace, patience, kindness, goodness, faithfulness, gentleness, self-control – all the fruit of the Spirit. This was my first experience of them in relation to the very character and nature of God. At the time it felt like I was there for days or even weeks, but eventually I got to the top and I fell on my face. I could not even look at the throne of God. I was just too overwhelmed. It was too awesome for me.

I was looking at the feet of God, when suddenly a thought came to me, "I wonder if there's a throne here that's mine?" So I crawled off, not looking up, and I saw Jesus sitting next to the Father, the Ancient of Days, and many, many thrones going off into the distance. I started crawling and then I got up and walked along, looking at the thrones. Most of them were not occupied, though just a few were, and some by people I recognised. I have been back since, and a whole lot more are occupied now.

I walked until I found my throne: it had my name on it, my heavenly name, which I so resonated with. It was not Mike, it was a description of who I am as a son of God; and I just knew it was my throne. So I sat on it and immediately I was next to Jesus. Even though I had walked for quite a long way to get there, I was immediately next to Jesus, next to the Father and Jesus. I was on His right hand side, so His right hand was holding my left hand but my right hand was free.

Suddenly I started to see heaven, and to see earth from a heavenly perspective, in a vision. Then I saw a portal that was open and the glory of God was being poured down through it. An angel came and took me into the atmosphere to show me what happens when portals get closed, because we empower the atmosphere of the earth to close off those everlasting doors that God has opened. The last thing I remember is thinking "I don't want to see those portals being closed." Then

I was back at my desk, and only about an hour had gone by in earthly time.

That was my first experience of these fire stones. It was totally overwhelming. The glory, the weight, the very essence, the nature, the character of the government of God was revealed through standing on those stones. That first time was an emotionally overload; I had no real cognitive process, it was just an awe-inspiring encounter that desperately made me want more.

Our sonship, our destiny, our glory and the essence and nature of the government of God which can outwork through us will be revealed to us by standing on the fire stones and experiencing the truth of who we are. As we ascend on those stones, they are a maturing of our relationship with God and our relationship to our sonship and destiny.

I do not know exactly what the role of the covering cherub would have been if he had not rebelled, but now he does not have that role. I know that now, we can engage and look into the arc of the presence of God ourselves, and we can also stand on those fire stones, walk on them and progress into maturity.

So my first encounter with the fire stones led me to engage the place where our thrones are, alongside the throne of God. We all have thrones, and we can all engage there, on our mountain in the realm of the kingdom of God, the highest realm in which I found that I could be seated. This is the place Paul is referring to when he says:

... and raised us up with Him, and seated us with Him in the heavenly places in Christ Jesus (Ephesians 2:6).

Later on, God had to remind me, "You need to come and spend more time here. Don't you remember what it was like when you were seated here and you saw things from a heavenly perspective?" I had been all caught up in what I was doing but I did not have the insight I needed to do it effectively. So He said, "Sit here, and look at this!" And all of

128

a sudden, everything looked different; everything changed. So I started to spend more time seated there and to allow what I could perceive and engage there to inform what I was doing in this realm; then I found I had more insight into how to legislate, how to govern and how to rule in my various spheres of responsibility.

Jesus is the light

In Him was life, and the life was the Light of mankind. The Light shines in the darkness, and the darkness did not grasp it... This was the true Light that, coming into the world, enlightens every person. He was in the world, and the world came into being through Him, and yet the world did not know Him. He came to His own, and His own people did not accept Him. But as many as received Him, to them He gave the right to become children of God, to those who believe in His name, who were born, not of blood, nor of the will of the flesh, nor of the will of a man, but of God (John 1:4-5, 9-13).

Jesus, as the Son of God, is the light that we focus on. He is the author and finisher of our faith, so we can connect to Him, the light of His glory can be revealed to us and we can be transfigured to radiate that glory and mature in our sonship. When we stand on the fire stones, we know that Jesus is the light of the world and that in Him was the light of life and the light of men: the light that shines in the darkness that the darkness cannot grasp, comprehend or overcome, the true light which is coming into the world which enlightens every person.

That is a really interesting statement. Jesus is the light that enlightens every person. That leaves no one out: Jesus, the light, is actually shining and working in every person to reveal the truth of who they are as sons of God, whether they yet know that or not.

Then Jesus again spoke to them, saying, "I am the Light of the world; the one who follows Me will not walk in the darkness, but will have the Light of life" (John 8:12).

129

Do all things without complaining or arguments; so that you will prove yourselves to be blameless and innocent, children of God above reproach in the midst of a crooked and perverse generation, among whom you appear as lights in the world... (Philippians 2:14-15).

We have the light of life: this light can be life to us and we can be this light to the world. Let us begin to embrace the light of the revelation which is contained within the fire stones, for our lives and for our destiny. In the garden, Man was sinless but not yet perfected: there would have been a process of ascension to attain maturity. Do not be concerned that 'ascension' has been put 'off limits' for most people who would call themselves Christians. Yes, much of what you will read online and elsewhere about the 'nine stages of ascension' has been perverted and twisted, but actually there is real truth in the concept of ascension into mature sonship.

We will not be led astray if we always begin by fixing our eyes on Jesus. Do not start with fixing your eyes on the fire stones, fix them on Jesus. He is the author and perfecter of our faith; He is the One who will unveil that light to us and in us. We engage the light, we arise and shine, and so we release that light.

We may be at level one, and we may only have engaged the stones in an emotional sense that brings us into a deeper revelation of the love, joy and peace of God but in time we will go deeper and higher and further than that. The nine fire stones really represent nine steps of ascension where we can each engage in maturity in sonship: nine steps to maturity.

The number nine represents the three-three-three of God: the fullness of the attributes of I AM, Father, Son and Spirit (three for each), that we can engage and from which we can receive revelation as we engage them; nine attributes of our sonship. The ninefold fruit of the Spirit reveals God's character to us: love, joy and peace, which is a representation of what Jesus brought here to the earth; patience, kindness and goodness, which is the Father's patience and tolerance with

130

us as His children; faithfulness, gentleness and self-control representing the Spirit. We are to be transformed into that same image, to bear that fruit. To be fruitful was the original call for Adam and Eve; their full fruitfulness would have come through maturing in their sonship.

Then there are nine strands of God's DNA, if you like, revealing His nature to us. The DNA attributes of God's revelation encoded within that light are justice, judgment and holiness for the Father; the way, the truth and the life for Jesus; and righteousness, peace and joy for the Spirit. And these are not just words, they are revelatory experiences of what it is to be righteous, what it is to live in peace, to be an expression of joy and so on.

So the first time I stood on the fire stones I experienced the fruit of the spirit. The next time it was the government of God (there are nine precepts that reveal God's government to us). And in subsequent encounters I have gone on into other, deeper things. I believe there are nine levels for each of the steps, so we can engage them nine times and get new revelation each time. And there will be more beyond that, but we will leave it there for now.

This is not something that you can go and just jump into straight away and go for the whole thing. The second time I went onto the fire stones, and I was not able to go back there until 2012, I was expecting to get more love, joy and peace. I took someone else with me because they asked me to. I had no mandate to do that, and they got wrecked by the experience, it was just too much for them. And much later, another of my encounters with the fire stones triggered the whole process of deconstruction of my mind, which is really not something to undertake lightly.

Psalm 119

During a 40-day fast in 2010, I had a dream. An angel came with this verse:

I am a stranger in the earth;
Do not hide Your commandments from me (Psalm 119:19).

I wondered what that was about and what it had to do with me. But God was trying to get me to see that I cannot get my government from earth or from the things of earth; I have to be first of all in heaven, and then from a heavenly perspective realise what the government of God is, and bring that to earth.

This dream prompted me to look up the first 40 verses of Psalm 119, which is the longest chapter in the Bible, with 176 verses. I had no idea what this meant, because I had not even been into heaven at this point:

How blessed are those whose way is blameless,
Who walk in the law of the Lord...

How can a young man keep his way pure?
By keeping it according to Your word.
With all my heart I have sought You;
Do not let me wander from Your commandments.
Your word I have treasured in my heart,
That I may not sin against You (Psalm 119:1, 9-11)

Even back then, I knew this was not talking about the Bible, but about a relationship with the Living Word of God. I meditated on these 40 verses and began to get a revelation of the characteristics of God's government. I received three 'nines': nine governmental truths, nine responses to truth and nine outworkings of truth.

- the law
- the testimonies
- the ways
- the precepts
- the statutes
- the commandments
- the judgments
- the ordinances
- the wonders of God.

Those were the aspects of government I saw in Psalm 119. I did not know then that they were going to feature in my future engagements on the fire stones, but I took them into my heart and nourished them, cherished them and set my heart upon them.

In those verses I found that you can:

- walk
- observe
- keep
- look, behold, seek
- learn, understand, take counsel
- speak
- meditate
- delight, desire, be diligent
- regard.

So when we get revelation, we need to take it seriously: as we allow it to begin to shape and transform our lives we will start to see results. We are going to be:

- blessed
- established
- not ashamed
- righteous
- thankful
- pure
- in abundance
- blameless
- revived.

These are all very good results that we would all like to see. And as I have engaged the fire stones in various revelations, I have experienced many of them as a consequence. It is not that I went around saying, "I want to be blessed, I want to be established." It was just that as I cherished these revelations in my heart, they have been outworking in my life.

The Joshua generation operates in the order of Melchizedek as forerunners of this heavenly royal priesthood to prepare the next, united generation to embrace their inheritance. As we operate from heavenly positions of government, we rule and legislate in intimacy and relationship with Father, Son and Spirit.

I did not really understand what precepts, statutes and laws were, or the difference between them. I imagined something like the 10 commandments: it is nothing to do with that. It is more like 'this is how God has made everything to work' and 'this is His very nature, by which He has brought everything into being.'

God's precepts are His very essence, the foundations upon which everything else is built, and can be transformational for you. His statutes are the way He sees everything: and the way He sees it brings order to it, in fact that is what brings it into being. His laws are how everything gets outworked: how creation exists, how we exist within creation. It is much more than simply 'you can do this and you can't do that.'

"Fire walk with Me"

Then I looked, and behold, in the expanse that was over the heads of the cherubim, something like a sapphire stone, in appearance resembling a throne, appeared above them (Ezekiel 10:1).

Ezekiel was trying to describe something he had no grid for. But we have the mandate to engage the fire which was in that sapphire stone (and each of the stones) to transform us into sonship. The Father said to me one day, "Fire walk with Me into transformation." I thought about that for a moment. Was I going to risk it? But I said, "Yes, okay. I'll be a living sacrifice." A living sacrifice is a dead man walking. It is as if you are dead to everything familiar but you are walking, you are alive to something completely different.

The fire is for the entrance into things, it gives us access. The purifying, refining fire of transformation is something we are all going to need to engage. Adam and Eve could have walked through that fire, through the fiery sword that was showing the way to the tree of life. In fact, many of their children did

(Adam and Eve had multiple children before they fell, who did not sin according to the sin of Adam. Some of them chose to follow Adam and remain on the earth but thousands of them went back into the realms of heaven, because Adam and Eve were producing children outside of time and space). We can engage with the fire today. In fact if we are going to fully enter into our sonship, fire is something to be embraced, not avoided.

The Father talked to me about how He is a consuming fire: "Son, I am all-consuming; there are no half-measures about Us. Our love is all-consuming; Our passion is all-consuming. I am an all-consuming fire: that means the way to intimacy is always the way of fire. So do not be afraid of the fire, whether it is the fiery sword, the fire on the mountain tops, the fiery altar, the river of fire, the stones of fire, the judgment seat of fire, or the place of fire [i.e. the place we thought was 'hell']: they are all expressions of My passion for you." So fire is part of our journey and part of embracing our sonship.

"My fire is never to be feared, but embraced as a powerful reminder; an expression of the commitment of My love and the revealing of just how far I am willing to go to secure relationship."

Jesus went through the fire of the cross; He went into the fire and preached the good news in the fire. I AM's fire offering was in place before the foundation of the earth. So when God decided to make creation, He had already put in place the fire of the sacrifice that was 'the Lamb that was slain before the foundation of the world', because He was never going to lose us. In the Mirror Bible, Francois Du Toit says that God found us in Christ before He ever lost us in Adam. That fire was in place before mankind's fall from the identity of sonship, to ensure our redeemed, restored, face-to-face innocence.

"Son, the so-called 'lake of fire' was another expression of my love, to end death and restore those who have fallen from their first estate. Son, follow the river of fire. Where does it go?"

As I say, sometimes I get so caught up with God and being with Him that I forget to look around and see what else is going on. I had been in the river of fire several times, but when He asked 'where does it go?' I had to go back to the river of fire and follow it to find out. I followed it all the way down to the lake of fire. The fire that flows from His throne is love; it flows from that realm into other realms which are figuratively called 'under the earth,' where it creates the lake of fire, into which it is continually flowing.

"Son, My throne is an expression of My authority as king; and the river of fire flows from My presence as an expression of love's government (which also expresses My love) to make the place where all can be restored, redeemed, reconciled who have not yet come through the fire of the cross. Only those of my children who refuse the invitation to come through Jesus, the door, choose to go there: and they can still be saved by fire."

In 1 Corinthians 3, Paul talks about the person who has no gold, silver and precious stones on their scroll, only wood, hay and stubble; and affirms that 'he himself will be saved, yet so as through fire' (v15). Some people object when I suggest that people can be 'saved' after death: but that is exactly what the apostle Paul says here, and the fire is instrumental in it.

"All get the choice before they die physically. No one will be able to have an excuse, because I speak to the hearts of all my children in many ways to offer them the choice." Everyone has the opportunity to choose, even if they have never heard of Jesus. God is in them: He is the light in them, and He is looking to reveal Himself to them.

"Son, you know that I AM is love, and We love Our children with a consuming, passionate, fiery love that cannot be escaped and will never give up or fail. The first fire stone of love is both a reminder of My very essence and My total commitment to My children's identity and destiny within I AM."

I would encourage you, when you finish reading this book, to go back over some of this and meditate further in it. Ask God about it for yourself, because you are not going to understand everything I have written just because you have read it once, nor should you just believe everything I am saying without checking it out with the Father for yourself. You may have seen some of my annual *Vision Destiny*[5] series, in which I used to share my journals from the previous year (until God told me to stop, towards the end of 2021). I guess that at the time I shared them I cognitively understood less than half of what I had written in my journals, but I knew that God had said it and that the revelation of it needed to be released.

I do not claim to understand everything, or know everything; but when God speaks to me, it stirs my spirit and I engage it; I let it captivate my heart. So when He says 'the first fire stone of love is a reminder of My very essence,' I know (because I have been there) that this really takes you deeper into God. And 'My total commitment to My children's identity and destiny,' shows how invested He is in us.

There are initially nine fire stones for us to engage, like steps, to ascend to the throne of the Ancient of Days, with Jesus at His right hand, and our thrones of sonship which are there too. And I believe there are at least nine levels of engagement for each stone. Rather than stepping on the first stone nine times, hoping to access every level of just one stone, I would recommend that you step on each of them one by one until you have stepped on all nine. Only return to them once you have been changed and transformed by the experience; and then re-engage and repeat the process, however long it takes. Do not try to rush it. It will take time if you really allow transformation to happen after each visit because the depth of revelation is not something that necessarily comes cognitively to your mind; it is received into the fabric of your

---

[5] See eg.freedomarc.org/vision-destiny

spirit and your being, and as your spirit digests it, your spirit then releases it to you as nourishment to enable you to grow.

I said that there are initially nine stones. In one engagement, the Father took me there and when I got to the top, He said, "Where's the next stone?" So I said, "There are only nine." And He said "No, there are supposed to be twelve." I thought to myself, "You don't expect me to make one, surely?" Then He showed me that when we, as mankind, would ascend to that place of maturity in sonship, we would release the next three stones; because there are nine stones on the covering cherub's body but twelve stones on the High Priest's breastplate, twelve stones that are the foundations of the New Jerusalem (which is us), and twelve stones which decorate the walls of the New Jerusalem. They are also connected to the pattern in which the tribes of Israel were arranged around the tabernacle when they camped in the wilderness (see the diagram below, or the colour version on the resources page).

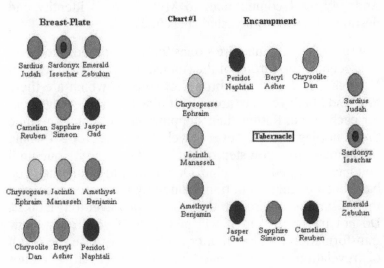

Breast-Plate   Chart #1   Encampment

Sardius Sardonyx Emerald
Judah Issachar Zebulun   Peridot   Beryl   Chrysolite
                                          Naphtali   Asher   Dan
                              Chrysoprase
                              Ephraim   Sardius
                                                                         Judah
Carnelian Sapphire Jasper
Reuben Simeon Gad   Tabernacle
                              Jacinth   Sardonyx
                              Manasseh   Issachar

Chrysoprase Jacinth Amethyst
Ephraim Manasseh Benjamin   Emerald
                              Amethyst   Zebulun
                              Benjamin
                                          Jasper   Sapphire Carnelian
Chrysolite Beryl Peridot   Gad   Simeon   Reuben
Dan Asher Naphtali

"Son, the first level of sonship reveals the emotional truth of the fruit of knowing Us intimately; and each level takes that foundation and builds upon it until My nature is revealed, which enables the fullness of My desire for Our sons to be like I AM.

Each level of experience and revelation builds upon love's essence to the full measure of the stature of the Son of God."

That is what will happen if we engage the fire stones and allow that engagement to change and transform us.

The completeness of Christ

...for the equipping of the saints for the work of service, to the building up of the body of Christ; until we all attain to the unity of the faith, and of the knowledge of the Son of God, to a mature man, to the measure of the stature which belongs to the fullness of Christ... but speaking the truth in love, we are to grow up in all aspects into Him who is the head, even Christ, from whom the whole body, being fitted and held together by what every joint supplies, according to the proper working of each individual part, causes the growth of the body for the building up of itself in love (Ephesians 4:12-13, 15-16).

That scripture refers to this process of coming to the fullness of our sonship. We have heard (and perhaps preached) all sorts of sermons around it without ever encountering love, so we have come up with all sorts of systems to try to outwork what Paul describes. It can only be achieved by engaging the deep love of God, experiencing it and letting it change us. In the Mirror Bible, verse 12 says:

Each expression of his gift is to fully equip and enable the saints for the work of the ministry so that they may mutually contribute in their specific function to give definition to the visible body of Christ (Ephesians 4:12 Mirror).

That is what this will do: it will present something on earth that represents the fullness of our sonship so that people can see what God is really like – in and through us. It goes on:

The purpose of these ministry gifts is to present everyone on par and in oneness of faith; believing exactly what the Son of God believes and knowing accurately what he knows concerning us. Standing face-to-face in equal stature to the measure of the completeness of Christ (Ephesians 4:13 Mirror).

Again, that is what this process is about: bringing us to that place of completeness in Christ, in our sonship. We are predestined to be conformed to that image – God has already decided it – but He wants us to cooperate in the process and embrace it.

Love gives truth its voice. The conversation that truth inspires creates the atmosphere wherein growth is both spontaneous and inevitable. The whole person is addressed in Christ who is the head of the body; he is the conclusion of God's communication with mankind (Ephesians 4:15 Mirror).

If you have not read scripture in this version, it sounds rather different to what we are accustomed to. The translator, Francois Du Toit, has adopted a process of returning to the root words to give us the relational aspect of what the Bible is saying. I would really encourage you to get a copy: it is a fantastic piece of literature that goes back to the original Greek and translates it within the framework of love. I highly recommend rereading the scriptures in this version (it is not the whole Bible yet, but as each book or set of books is completed they are being added). As you read, allow the truth of it to really resonate with you.

I gave up reading the Bible in English versions like the NASB and the NIV a few years ago, because they just did not reflect what I was seeing when I met God. Do not misunderstand me: I use the Bible all the time, especially when speaking, preaching or writing. I have read it so much that I carry it in me. Literal versions, though much harder to read, were more in keeping with the God I was meeting. But when I started to read the Mirror Bible, it totally inspired me to engage it again, and it breathes new life into me to read these kinds of words:

From him flows the original composition and detail of our design like words entwined in poetry, they connect layer upon layer to complete the harmony, following the rhythm of his thoughts like footprints. Meanwhile the body thrives and pulsates with the energy of love. Each individual expression finds its complete measure there (Ephesians 4:16 Mirror).

Fire, love and creative light

"I kept looking
Until thrones were set up,
And the Ancient of Days took His seat;
His vesture was like white snow
And the hair of His head like pure wool.
His throne was ablaze with flames,
Its wheels were a burning fire.
A river of fire was flowing
And coming out from before Him..." (Daniel 7:9-10a)

This is why I encourage us all to embrace the fire stones, to engage the consuming fire of God's presence in love. God is a consuming fire (see Hebrews 12:29), and the fire stones are a really intense expression of the very nature and character of God in that consuming fire aspect.

"Son, the fire stones are the stones of destiny where the fire of Our DNA is encoded within the stones. The stones were created to release the light of our character and nature as the precepts that were to be reflected out into all creation, to enable all to be connected to the source. The waves of light that revealed the essence of pure love could be absorbed by all spirit and form the particles of love's manifestation within the creation as the building blocks of all things.

"The light-bearer refused to reflect the light, choosing to create darkness by reflecting an absence of Our presence. All those who followed him became darkness, and introduced darkness into creation. My sons are called to be sons of light; to arise and shine; to restore light to creation by absorbing into themselves Our image across all spectrums and all frequencies, releasing and radiating love's light.

"As My sons embrace the light of each stone at each level, deep will truly reveal the depths and manifoldness of who We really are and so will be able to be a true reflection of fire; transcendence converging as the immanence. The destiny of

141

all My sons is encoded within Us and can be experienced by engaging the stones of the fire of Our precepts."

That is why and how we are to be a light to the world. We could spend a year meditating on what God said there and never exhaust the revelation it contains. But ultimately He is saying that whatever is in Him (in eternity) He wants to converge in us (in time) to reveal what eternity is like; for the manifoldness, the multicoloured, multifaceted, multi-nature of God to be revealed.

"The willingness to embrace the consuming fire of Our love and be purified and refined is the precursor to engaging the stones and being able to receive the deep revelation of eternal sonship. Created and creative light will form an interference pattern and cancel each other out, leaving darkness. By engaging the fire stones, you are bathing in the creative revelation light that will activate the creative light hidden within the fabric of your being. It will radiate from your innermost being, transforming created light back to creative light so that you can radiate the glory of sonship once again."

The created light that we are now familiar with is not the light we were birthed with; and it is not the light that our spirit was created in. We are to be light here, to bring true light back into creation itself – and there is so much dark energy and dark matter out there – but our light will bring the groaning of creation back into harmony. Creative light has multiple spectrums: not just the seven colours of the rainbow but all the multi-coloured multi-frequencies of light.

"The created order has been separated from the creative realm and is longing to be reconnected and brought back into the harmony of the first estate from which it was removed by the choice of my son Adam to abandon the light of life and walk in the darkness of self. As my sons choose to walk in the creative light of their sonship, creation will again respond to love's light. Creation itself is waiting for you to arise and shine by discovering the true nature of your sonship deep within us. Son, true ascension is not entering through the veil into the heavenly realms: it is entering into Us to ascend in the maturity of your sonship."

True Ascension

"True ascension is becoming mature sons by embracing the nine stones of the nine levels; that will add the last three stones of sonship to reach and live from the eternal now. There were always intended to be twelve stones that would take the thrones of sonship from [the realm of] Heaven to the place 'high above all authority,' through the [realms of] Heaven of Heavens and Perfection, to [the realm of] Eternity."

So where we are seated now (or can be), in the realm of Heaven, will be raised up to another level, taken up into the Heaven of Heavens (which is where the *Ya Sod* of God is, and other courts). Then the next stone will take them up into the realm of Perfection (where the Person of God is, hidden in the dark cloud) and then to the realm of Eternity. Then we will all be seated at the highest place, along with Jesus and the Father. But we get to be involved in that process.

"This is where the speed of light is the closest to the purity of eternity's perfection within the circle of love's dance. Son, this is the highest estate within the created order of the Creator that can be ascended to. Son, the stones of destiny will reconnect your past, present and future destiny into wholeness, remove all separation from within your being, and bring a clarity to your true identity and calling as my sons. Heaven is the centre, where your thrones of sonship are currently positioned; but as my sons ascend, so will the thrones ascend to the highest place within the created order."

Let us look again at that passage in Zechariah:

"Thus says the LORD of hosts, 'If you will walk in My ways and if you will perform My service, then you will also govern My house and also have charge of My courts, and I will grant you free access among these who are standing here'" (Zechariah 3:7).

143

To ascend, we need to go through this process of friendship and walking in His ways, performing His service, having access to the courts and assemblies of God and beyond.

In this realm, in the Kingdom of Earth, we are servants, stewards and friends, walking in His ways.

In the Kingdom of God realm, we are lords who govern the house.

In the Kingdom of Heaven, we are kings who take charge of the courts.

In the realm of Heaven, we are sons who have access in the assemblies and councils of God.

In the realm of the Heaven of Heavens, we come into full co-heirship.

In the realm of Perfection we begin to be co-creators.

In the realm of Eternity we will be ascended fathers.

We will fulfil many different roles and positions as we mature and ascend in sonship. This is not necessarily all going to happen in this age, some may be for the ages to come, but unless we ascend to the place where we are functioning in sonship, we are not going to be able to go any further. Our ascension is integral to God's plan to go beyond the restoration of all things to their original condition, into the condition they would have reached if they had continued to develop as God intended, and had never needed restoring.

Our eventual ascension will be into realms higher than we can currently be seated in. We can go into those places: I have been into Perfection and even into Eternity, to engage with the Person of God rather than just His Presence (which is what we engage in the other realms), but until we mature further in our sonship we cannot yet be seated there.

Successive encounters

Engaging love, joy, peace, patience, kindness, goodness, faithfulness, gentleness and self-control on the fire stones is a good place to start, but we do not have to stop there. In my first encounter in 2008, I engaged with the fruit of God's character at a level I had never experienced before, and it increased my desire to pursue intimacy: once I had experienced that, nothing else on earth could ever match it. I was desperate to get back there.

When I did eventually return in 2012, I had a revelation of the character of God relating to Kingdom government: His laws, testimonies, and ways, His precepts, statutes and commandments, His judgments, ordinances and wonders.

My third encounter was in 2013, and took me literally into the stones: on the first two occasions I stood on them, but in this third encounter I was enveloped into them. That took me into a level of the fruit of the nature of God that went deeper into me, not just touching my emotions but every particle of the fabric of my being. It connected me to God's love for all His children and changed my perspective of looking at creation. The earlier encounters had been all about me: feeling love, feeling joy, feeling peace; and then I saw God's government and realised we had some role to fulfil in that. This time I was encountering those fruits, but in a completely different way, directed outwards. Being absorbed into the stones was significant of the fact that this was an even deeper experience for me.

I had to access the fourth encounter, in 2014, by a different way, walking into the river of fire first (an intense experience in itself) before I could even get to the fire stones. This time they revealed a whole new level of my sonship: my identity, my position and my legislative authority. As I stood on the fourth step, Wisdom came to me and gave me a chancellor's seal and a staff. That opened up a whole new range of experiences: I was able to engage the twelve Chancellors' houses; I was able to access Satan's trophy room; I was able to go through the doors on Wisdom's Heights, and into the stars, into the atmosphere of the earth.

Everything opened up, because I had been given a role which carried greater authority, a level of authority I could not have borne without my previous encounters with the fire stones. I needed to be transformed before I could be entrusted with a chancellor's seal and staff, which would eventually open up for me a new way of engaging.

My fifth encounter was in 2015. This was my initial access into the essence of God's nature and government from an eternal perspective. It took me back into His eternal heart, outside of time and space. I had touched on this in previous encounters, but this really showed me how much we need to be there, to administrate from there, and to live from that place. It created a deeper desire for that eternal aspect of God and opened up access to the ancient pathway and the four faces of God in a completely different way.

In my sixth encounter, in 2016, the Father took me to the stones and walked on them with me; that brought me into a deeper sense of the Father's heart and mind. It was a really powerful encounter, in preparation for my deconstruction. This was the time He asked me about the next stone.

My seventh was in 2018, during an activation in the session of the *Sons Arise! Engaging The Father* conference which corresponds with this chapter. That encounter began to unveil some of the shifts I was to go through over the next few years. Over the course of subsequent encounters I have seen the three further stones manifest and walked on them, as I have described in the *Vision Destiny* videos and *The Eschatology of the Restoration of All Things* book.

The unveiling of these new dimensions and realities have revealed mankind's need for further ascension and provided me with a glimpse into the ages to come. I have been curious about what the ages to come entail and I have seen some of the mysteries that are hidden in the discovery room of the

Chancellors' houses, but I did not really get a proper sense of what it would be like until God took me and showed me the other levels of sonship that we would come into, and what is involved in our co-heirship and co-sonship.

Activation #9: Engage the fire stones

My journey to discover my true identity and eternal destiny has been accelerated by engaging the fire stones. As I look back and see how significant these encounters have been for me, both in my relationship with the Father and in recognising my governmental responsibility as a son, I want to give you the opportunity of engaging the fire stones for yourself. If you have engaged them before, then return to them and be willing to go to whatever is the next level for you.

I can only share what my experiences have been. Please do not try to copy them: you can have your own experiences which will be tailored especially for you. There are different kinds and levels of experiences you may have when you go there; your encounters may be very different from mine.

Such engagements are open for all of us when we are pursuing sonship, because without them we are not going to ascend in that sonship. The revelation is there for us to experience. However, I am not going to guarantee that you can go to the fire stones today, as I do not know where you are personally in your own walk. We are going to ask Jesus to take you where you need to go. Trust Him to do that. If you are able to go there then just embrace the process (it may or may not be cognitive). If He takes you somewhere else, go with Him. It will be the right place for you to go at this time.

If you are going to the fire stones, you are going into the fire of God's presence. Allow it to come around you, embrace you and consume you. Each stone will be an experience that will bring change and transformation for you.

Again, either read through the text first
and then engage, or use the audio
recording (by scanning the QR code with
your phone camera or visiting the
resources page online).

Heaven is open.
Close your eyes and step into the
realm of heaven.

Relax, and set your heart's desire on sonship
and engaging the Father.
Step through the veil and ask Jesus, as your high priest,
to engage you
and take you to those fire stones of destiny
- or wherever is right for you.

Let Him lead you there.
He may take you in various ways,
but just engage your spirit with it,
set the desire of your heart towards it,
and let Him take you through
whatever veil you need to go through
to whatever place you need to engage.

When you come before the river of fire,
leading up to the throne of God,
take a step – by faith, if you can't see it.

Choose to take a step onto the first stone.
Allow whatever you experience
to totally captivate your heart.
Let your whole being be immersed in the love of God.
Whenever you are ready,
allow Jesus to walk you up those steps.

You may want to stay on one: that is okay.
You may want to step on each one of them.
Eventually you may even get to the throne of God

and find your throne there.

But let this be a time when your whole being begins to
engage in the revelation of the light of your sonship
that is contained within those stones
that reveal the depth of the Father's heart
and reveal who you are in relationship with Him.

If you ascend those steps,
you may want to find your throne,
find your new name, the name that God imparts to you,
and take your place
seated in this place of heavenly authority as a son of God
alongside the Father and the Son...

Even if you were not cognitively aware of it, your spirit will
have been receiving as you engaged. Allow the fullness of what
you have received to begin to change and transform you, to
bring you into agreement and release the wholeness that
comes through these encounters. Remember, this is just a first
encounter and there can be many more to come.

It may take some time for all this to outwork. Do not rush it
or try to force it; be nourished and nurtured in your sonship
as the revelation of those stones gets continually reflected out
to bring you into that place within the heart of God as a son
of God.

11. Times of Refreshing

In the beginning

In the beginning God... (Genesis1:1a).

That is a really good place to start, for all of us to connect with God, as He was in the beginning, is, and always will be. I believe God wants to bring us back to when we were a thought, a desire in His heart, when He looked at us and He drew us into that perfect relationship of Father, Son and Spirit, totally relating to one another and with no need for anything else. But His love was not just selfish: to be a really full expression of love, that love has to be given, and He always had us in His heart, in His desire.

Love, joy and peace were perfectly expressed in that relationship and when I began to reconnect with it, it transformed both my understanding and my outworking of love.

In the beginning was the Word, and the Word was with God, and the Word was God (John 1:1).

To go back to the very beginning is to find the Word already present there; face to face with God. The Word is I am; God's eloquence echoes and concludes in him. The Word equals God (John 1:1 Mirror).

That passage is referring to Jesus, and if you look at the word 'with' in Greek (*pros*) it actually means 'face to face', as Francois Du Toit brings out in the Mirror Bible translation, not just alongside someone. Face to face is a completely different dynamic because you are looking into the person's eyes and seeing their expression; you are picking up their intentions and emotions. So Jesus was (and is) face to face with the Holy Spirit and face to face with the Father: they are not first of all outward-looking, they are looking in toward each other. Then when they invite us into that place of relationship, we are looking at them and they are looking at us; and we are not stationary, we are in a dance of love that is

150

in motion, it is active, it is alive, it is living. They are not just staring at each other for eternity: there is life in it, and we are invited into that life.

Times of refreshing

"Therefore repent and return, so that the sins may be wiped away, in order that times of refreshing may come from the presence of the Lord; and that He may send Jesus, the Christ appointed for you, whom heaven must receive until the period of restoration of all things about which God spoke by the mouth of His holy prophets from ancient time" (Acts 3:19-21).

When Peter talks here about the sins being washed away, that is Adam's choice to go his own way, not the things we do wrong. Doing things wrong is just the consequence of losing our identity. So when we agree with God (and that is what 'repentance' really means, an agreement of mind with God) about who we are, we are reconnecting to our original identity. If we truly come back into agreement with the mind of God, if we return to God's original thought and intention about us, that will restore our identity.

Our old (DIY, do-it-yourself) way of being is wiped away because we have returned to the place of identity and relationship, having intimacy with the presence of the Lord, being intimate with Him face-to-face, knowing the mind of God and the vast sum of His thoughts about us. We are seeing Him (and seeing ourselves in Him). We are beholding Him and being transformed into the image that we are seeing, as He shares with us who He always created us to be. Having that intimacy of relationship, we will be refreshed as those times of refreshing come from the presence of the Lord.

In our worship services, sometimes the presence of the Lord comes and we feel refreshed; there is an aspect to that which is great, but that 'refreshing' is not really what this passage is talking about. It goes way beyond having a nice cup of cool water, it is actually referring to being able to catch your breath again, having restored breath, restored life. The Greek word is *anapsyksis*, which Strong's tells us means "breathe easily (again), hence, refreshing, cooling, or reviving with fresh air. A recovery of breath, a refreshing..."

Breathe

Then the Lord God formed man of dust from the ground, and breathed into his nostrils the breath of life; and man became a living being (Genesis 2:7).

When Adam was created, God breathed into him and he became a living being, a living soul. Adam derived all of his life from the Father's breath; and I would suggest that we have probably been breathing in atmospheres that are not the Father's breath. God wants to restore us and breathe into us again the words and truth and essence of who we are. For that to happen we cannot be turned away from Him, we have to be face to face, which is why He is calling us back to that place of intimacy within His heart within eternity.

Then in his sermon Peter goes on to speak about restoration, specifically mentioning that it has been prophesied from ancient time. Right from the very beginning, God has been looking to bring us back to the place where we would be restored and He could breathe back into us.

And when He had said this, He breathed on them and said to them, "Receive the Holy Spirit" (John 20:22).

In effect, Jesus was saying, "Receive your life back again because now you are alive in Me; and you were born from above, you are in a totally new, restored relationship. You are not coming to Me through any legal, law-based system: this is face-to-face intimacy, fatherhood and sonship restored. So I am going to breathe back into you your restored sonship, who you were always intended to be, and if you keep breathing from this source you are going to be refreshed continually and will continually know who you are. But if you turn away to another source, you are going to be breathing in something which is not going to refresh you and give you life."

That is how important it is for us to stay in that place of face to face intimacy. It is wonderful when we come together corporately and sense His presence: where two or three are gathered He is in the midst. But we do not need a corporate gathering for this refreshing: this comes from our personal, face-to-face relationship. Then when we come together corporately we will be bringing all our face-to-face relationships and multiplying the refreshing in an atmosphere exponentially filled with His presence; because when we breathe out, we are breathing out the same refreshing presence of God to each other.

Freely we have received, freely give. I am not going to breathe in, hold my breath and keep it to myself until all the oxygen is expended: I have to breathe out. When we are intimate with God and encounter Him face to face, it is always going to be expressed outwardly to others, otherwise it would be selfish. But we need to receive it and breathe in before we can breathe out; and once we have breathed out, we have to breathe back in again, otherwise we have nothing to breathe out. It is the continual, ongoing breath of life.

If you think of the name of God, *Yod Hei Vav Hei*, that actually sounds like the breathing in and breathing out process. We have to be face to face for that refreshing presence to come, so that there is a restoration of what was in the beginning, when Adam was able to walk in the realms of the Father and the Father walked in the realms of Adam, so they had a kind of overlapping relationship. And there is so much more even than that, which we need to be restored.

Activation #10: Breathe

I suggest you take a few minutes now to engage with the Father face to face; let Him embrace you and breathe into you. Relax, and do not strive to make anything happen, just allow Him to engage you. You can read the text or

scan the QR code to follow the audio from the resources webpage.

Instead of asking Him to come here, into this realm, engage Him in your spirit, in that 'first love' place where you have invited Him in; in that place in your spirit where He can breathe life back in again.

Just begin to think about this
and think about the Father's presence
and the wind of His presence
and the breath of His presence
and being face-to-face with Him.

Let all this begin to form in your imagination
and then engage with it.

First of all, if you have not opened your first love gate
today, just choose to open that door.
Invite the Father's presence
and let Him face-to-face
begin to breathe His breath into you.

And breathe it in.

As He is breathing into you
He is breathing words of life, living words.
He is breathing into you your identity.
He is breathing into you your sonship.

He is releasing into you, in His very breath,
the vast sum of His thoughts about you;
calling you to your original identity
in face-to-face intimacy with Him.

Let Him breathe it in.
Receive it.
Be refreshed.

...

God said
"Let us make man in our image,
according to our likeness..."
(Genesis 1:26 [part]).

So just receive His image
and being restored to His likeness.

And God blessed them...
(Genesis 1:28 [part]).

Let God bless you with His life
with His empowerment to prosper and to succeed.

And God said "be fruitful...."
(Genesis 1:28 [part]).

Receive the capacity to be fruitful,
to multiply,
to fill your spheres of government;
to subdue and rule
over all you have been given in sonship.

Let that empowerment be breathed in you
through His refreshing presence;
His very living words,
breathed into your whole physical being, soul and spirit.

I would encourage you every day, when you open your first love gate, to just let Him breathe into you all the life that you need for that day. And then you can breathe out and breathe in throughout the rest of the day, being conscious of the face-to-face relationship you have. You are not separated from Him, you can be consciously aware of His presence and continually aware that you are drawing from Him and releasing; that you are not giving away your own strength, you are receiving and then giving from what you received.

155

12. Four Faces of God

Esteem, value and worth

Francois Du Toit says[6]:

"Jesus did not do what He did to reconcile God with us; this is Father, Son and Spirit clothed in human skin, lovingly and willingly going to the gruesome extreme of a ridiculously unfair trial by a human court, and the scandalous execution of innocent life, in order to persuade us most convincingly of their priceless esteem of us and their relentless love for us, and to forever rescue our minds from every definition of unworthiness and condemnation, and every sense of separation.

"In the broken, bleeding body of Jesus, the incarnate Engineer of the universe willingly dies humanity's death at the hands of his own creation in order to redeem our minds from the plague of a sin-consciousness that left us distanced and indifferent for ages and generations, stuck in the wilderness of our self-help religious and survival programs."

Perhaps we tend to think that God looks at us and finds fault in what He sees. He does not. He looks at us and has 'priceless esteem' for us. That is what the cross was about: restoring us to face-to-face intimacy so that we would value ourselves the way God values us. Self-esteem and self-worth are what we get from doing things ourselves. Esteem, worth and value come from Him. So when we see ourselves as He sees us, and feel and know how valuable we are to Him, we can realise how valuable we are to the creation for which He has given us responsibility.

From the beginning, everything was about engaging God in relationship. God and Adam walked together in perfect

---

[6] Francois Du Toit: *The Mirror Bible*, Hebrews Chapter 12 Extended Notes: Extended Notes on the Blood - Hebrews 12:24.

fellowship. When Adam and Eve messed up, what did God say? Not "What have you done?" but "Where are you?" He wanted them to come back into fellowship with Him.

That did not work out, so Adam fell from the realm where he could walk with God in Eden and God's heavenly garden. It was by his choice. He could have accessed the fiery way to the Tree of Life but he chose to do his own thing. So God came to earth Himself in the person of Jesus, the Son of Man, who represented us to restore that walking relationship, that fellowship, that face-to-face innocence, esteem, value and worth. And in that restored relationship, God is transforming us into His image.

Four faces

In Ezekiel chapter 1, the prophet describes a human form that had four dimensional faces of lion, ox, eagle and man. This is not the same as the four creatures before the throne in Revelation, which do not have human form, and only have one face each. In Ezekiel, this is a description of someone who has been transformed by the face of God to carry four faces. This is a vision of us.

God wants us to see that when we are restored to His image and who He created us to be, it carries the fullness of the faces of God and the four aspects of His government. The lion, the ox and the eagle represent the Father, Son and Spirit; and God has created us as man to reflect His fullness. As we saw, there are not only the original nine fire stones, but a further three stones, making twelve. Now we are included in the fullness of His government. He has given us the authority to govern the universe with Him in perfect face-to-face relationship in which those faces are continually living and active.

Four living creatures

Then in Revelation chapter 5 we have a description of the four living creatures:

157

In the centre, around the throne, were four living creatures, and they were covered with eyes, in front and behind. The first living creature was like a lion, the second was like an ox, the third had a face like a man, the fourth was like a flying eagle. Each of the four living creatures had six wings and was covered with eyes all round, even under its wings. Day and night they never stop saying: "Holy, holy, holy is the Lord God Almighty, who was, and is, and is to come" (Revelation 4:6-8 NIV).

"Holy, holy, holy" references Father, Son and Spirit. "Who was, and is, and is to come" references the eternal nature of His purpose. God wants us to be brought into that alignment. Three is the number of government and four is a window. The four living creatures represent each of the governmental faces of God: Father, Son, and Spirit; with the fourth face that of the man in priestly agreement, in order to open up a window for manifestation.

God has designed His government to require the agreement of man to open up heaven and come to earth. He has given us the final say: for as long as we continue to say that we want to do things our own way, we will not see heaven manifested on the earth. Heaven is only going to be manifested on earth again when we start to say, "I am now in agreement with the likeness of who You made me to be: my heart is connected to Your heart, and I have the heart of the Father. I know Your heart from eternity, and I am now in the place in heaven where I can begin to legislate and govern and be a gateway into the earth." Then the glory of God will fill the earth; the kingdom of God will fill the earth, and on into other dimensions, because 'of the increase of His government and peace there will be no end.' (See Isaiah 9:7).

So the Arc of God's presence governmentally manifests as four faces: lion, ox, eagle and man. They represent the kingly, the oracle (the prophetic), the legislator (the apostolic) and the priestly. They are all represented in the name of God, YHVH, so when you stand in that place you stand in the name of God. We have access to the name of God, being in His name, and therefore we are to represent all four faces as sons.

158

We are all named within Him and He carries our names within Him. So we stand in His name and in the name that we have in His name. And He has the vast sum of His thoughts about every one of our names within Him, so that when we look into His face we see reflected our name in Him. This is why it is so important for us to be face to face with Him and to look into His face. It is also why religion will stop us looking at God face to face, because "if you look at God face to face, you will die." Yes, that is what it says in Genesis 32:30, but we come through Jesus, who has made the way for us. He is the door by which we enter: His flesh is torn, and the veil is torn. He is our high priest; He has made us righteous and given us a ring of sonship. Therefore we can draw near and come to that place of engaging the four faces of God in intimacy.

This is where the government of God is outworked. In the earthly tabernacle the high priests would sing or chant the names of God, *Yod Hei Vav Hei*, and a window would open in heaven; and God would manifest His presence in the portal between the wings of the cherubim as the high priest engaged with the name of God. So God's presence, the *'Shekinah* glory' would appear between the arc of the two wings. Now, in the New Covenant, heaven is open and we are all called to go in and engage God for ourselves.

When I first started engaging around the arc of the presence of God, I was not looking for that manifest presence of God – and in fact I could not see it. I was just interested in finding out what the will of God was for me every day, getting the manna, and having my heart written on so that I could go and 'do'. Eventually God dealt with my soul so that I could sense and see. Once I saw the four faces, I was always drawn to the Eagle to start with. I avoided the man, the priestly, because I really did not think it was my kind of thing. But soaring, looking, seeing the bigger picture and how it all fits together: awesome! And then I started getting drawn to the king (the lion), and then the ox.

Only later did I finally discover what it would have been better to engage with from the first, the man, which was my priestly role. If I had engaged with the man first, I would have seen that in that priestly role I could step into God and go back into eternity. I spent a year or two going round the lion, ox and eagle, avoiding going back into eternity because I was not accepting my role as a priest. But, in the end, I did eventually engage the man.

Engaging the Arc

We can all draw near to this place, the Holy of Holies in the heavenly tabernacle, to engage the Arc. Until we take our place as a royal priest we do not have anything to administrate into the earth. We have tried to do the apostolic and the prophetic on the earth without being a royal priest in heaven; and therefore we only have earthly manifestations such as spiritual gifts, rather than a heavenly manifestation of the fullness of our sonship.

We form an arc in heaven when we come into that place. We are that king and priest, so we form an agreement in heaven to receive the revelation of the Father's heart and that opens a window for heaven to come into the earth. Then when it comes into the earth we form another arc on the earth of agreement between the apostle and prophet (or the oracle and legislator). I use the terms 'oracle' and 'legislator' because 'apostle' and 'prophet' have connotations of fivefold ministry gifts, which is not what this is. Because we have agreed as a priest and a king in heaven to receive the revelation of the Father's heart and then to administrate it, we carry that eternal word and we become its living expression on the earth; then that word is legislated and outworked.

This is very different from what we would traditionally think of as 'apostles' and 'prophets'. We are used to prophets who speak a prophecy: this is not about speaking, but being a living demonstration of the living word that we carry.

... God's household, having been built on the foundation of the apostles and prophets ... (Ephesians 2:19b-20a).

160

If the household is built on the foundation of the apostles and prophets, where is that foundation? In the ground, in the dirt. It does not say that the apostles and prophets are the roof of the house, providing a 'covering', as many apostolic and prophetic ministries claim to do. The foundation is in the earth. Then there is an arc between heaven and earth, as king and priest come into agreement with oracle and legislator.

So the heavenly Bench of Three, Father, Son and Spirit, the government of heaven, produce blueprints for each of us. We have a destiny scroll, a blueprint for our lives. For everything God wants to see manifested on the earth as an expression of heaven; for every ekklesia and for every embassy of heaven, there is a blueprint. When we agree as the priest and king, the light of God shines on that blueprint and it produces a shadow on the earth. If we do not agree, there is no light and no shadow.

There is a sequence: an agreement, an arc in heaven, to agree the blueprint (across the top of this diagram); then an arc between heaven and earth to see that blueprint manifested on earth (down the right hand side of the diagram); and finally an

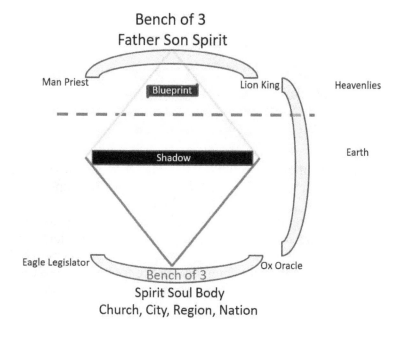

arc of agreement on earth to lay the foundation for what is to manifest here (across the bottom of the diagram).

Up to now, the apostles and prophets have been trying to get a vision out of heaven and build it on the earth. The light of God has not produced a shadow, instead they have produced a vision in their own image. When the light of God does produce a shadow, you then have the reflection of God's government, which is the bench of three on earth, at the foundation. The building can be established on the foundation and occupy the shadow. Foundational government releases people as living stones to be built up on earth. That blueprint is from heaven, and we need to have agreement on earth.

That is when you start to see heaven manifested on earth. But most of us did not know how to do that so we have just done the best we could. Unfortunately, our best has been to build mountains, hierarchical structures of mediatorial coverings.

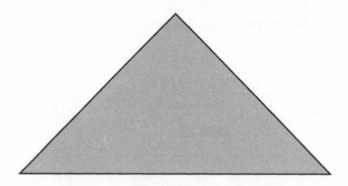

We are not supposed to build a mountain on earth like that: anything we build is supposed to be the other way up. How far can people get with this model? Only as far as the top of that pinnacle (and there are already people there who will make sure you stay in your place, and do not take theirs). If we build the other way up, a foundation will release people to go up, and wider and wider, because there is no end to the increase of His government and peace.

Mostly we imagine that if God is going to manifest, He is going to look like the Father, or like Jesus. When I first started thinking about coming before the throne, dressed in my royal robes, I was expecting that manifestation of God's Presence. What I saw instead was the manifestation of the four faces of God, which was quite a surprise. But when I did experience that manifestation, that is when I got drawn into engaging the four faces and their truth began to be unveiled.

When we engage God's presence in that tabernacle, we start by engaging His name, *Yod Hei Vav Hei*. Here at Freedom, there was a season in which we found that we were singing that name a lot when we worshipped: we would get to a point where we had entered into something and we would sing His name over and over, because His name was manifesting the revelation of His government to change things here. When we come into agreement with Him there, that then changes things here.

We engage with the seven spirits of God, the four living creatures and the four angels of transformation (as we did in chapter 4, when we used the diagrams of flags and banners as a physical representation of what we were looking to engage with spiritually). Our intention is to have heaven and earth completely overlap, so that it is as if we are here, but we are there; we are living here, and we are living there; we are walking in two realms at the same time and living from the perspective of dual (or even multiple) realms. Then we find that heaven and earth become more and more in agreement as change begins to take place on earth to align with heaven.

We engage the heavenly Tabernacle, the Holy of Holies, the Arc of God's presence: to engage inwards, as a priest; to administrate outwards, as a king; to come into an arc of agreement. Then as the oracle we carry inwards what we have received in the intimacy of God's Word; and as a legislator we legislate it outwards. Within this there is the same rhythm of life, of the breath: I breathe in; I breathe out; I breathe in; I breathe out. I breathe in in heaven; I breathe out in heaven. I breathe in on earth; I breathe out on earth.

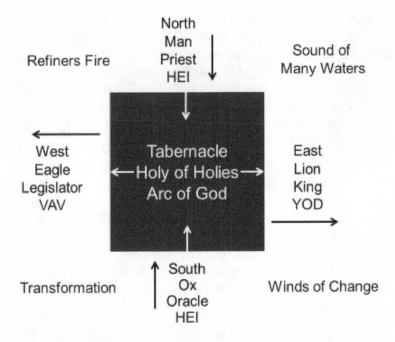

Engaging with the four angels can help us to connect with the process of being transformed into that image, because we need the fire of refining to purify some of the things that stop us looking like who God created us to be: our image has likely been distorted by what we thought and felt about ourselves rather than what He feels and says about us. A distorted image does not accurately reflect God, so He has sent these four orders of angels to help the Joshua generation to transition from an earthly to a heavenly perspective; from an old to a new perspective; from the perspective of engaging God here to engaging God there. Winds of Change is the angel assigned to administer all this, to bring us into a new dimension of relationship and identity for a new season.

The name of God is an intrinsic part of this process, and we can step into His name and become part of the process rather than just an observer. When you step into something, you can then look out from within; everything takes on a different perspective when you are not looking at it from an earthly perspective anymore.

I can stand in and see through the eyes of the lion: seeing all the government that needs to be in place. I can speak with the authority of the lion's voice, which is a roar because it carries with it a frequency that changes things.

I can stand in and look from the eyes of the ox: seeing things from the perspective of God's eternal word. I can look and say "This doesn't look like His eternal word, this needs to be changed and transformed and aligned into His eternal word."

When I first looked from heaven to the earth, I saw the realm that I live in here. I saw it from God's perspective, and it was the most amazing, beautiful vision, a multicoloured, vibrant ultra-ultra-high definition 3D picture. And then He showed me what I normally see. I was so disappointed, because it was grey and dull and lifeless. And He said, "Well, this is what life looks like to you from on earth, but look what it looks like when you see through My eyes! This is My view of what life is and what I intend it to be."

That is what we want to see here on earth, rather than "Well, we just get by, and it's hard and it's difficult..." Life is not difficult when you see it from a heavenly perspective. Of course you then have to work it out, which can indeed be difficult because we have to go through the process of change to align ourselves with what God sees there, so we can be that here.

When we stand in His name, it becomes *Yod Hei Shin Vav Hei*. The Hebrew letter *Shin* comprises three strokes, and it stands for us: body, soul and spirit. We are in the name of God, carrying His power of attorney and His full authority and power as a son made in His image.

Arcs of agreement

In a visionary experience, in our main meeting room at the Freedom Centre (which happens to face east), I saw the four living creatures standing in the east, south, west and north sides of the room. Each had a trumpet and a standard; they had come to herald a new level of sonship, into which we can

165

mature. In the centre was Urandiel, our church angel, carrying a standard bearing an image of the four faces of God; fire was coming off him, releasing fresh passion for the Father. He was urging us to come into this place of agreement and alignment.

Then I saw the four living creatures move around the room creating a vortex of colour, sound and energy that opened the heavens. In a new dimension I saw more angels assigned. I saw the seven spirits of God, and the cloud of witnesses with mantles of all kinds of different colours, all looking to engage with us. It was a powerful encounter, and it is still available for us all to enter into and engage with, because it was not just for us as a local ekklesia, but for the whole Joshua generation.

I saw it in the spiritual realm, but I also saw it as a prophetic act we could outwork in this realm, which is why we started laying out flags on the floor and moving around the room to stand on the different flags to help us engage with what they represent, as I described earlier.

Any two faces can form an arc of agreement with one another. So the faces form arcs of agreement between themselves for government, and windows of engagement, to open portals. Everything that is an agreement of two opens up a window to experience something: they agree, and something manifests. I spent probably about six weeks every Sunday going and standing in a different place. We did not have the flags out but I could see where Winds of Change was standing and where the lion was, so I went and stood in the arc between them. I found myself going through a portal and engaging something in heaven as well as experiencing something on earth. Over the weeks I went around each of them connecting up with the different arcs and I discovered that they took me places and opened up new experiences for me and gave me revelation. You do not need to be in our building in Barnstaple to engage with this: you can step into it wherever you are.

Engaging with Winds of Change is the breath of God bringing in a new season; engaging Sound of Many Waters is engaging His voice, a vibrational frequency which will bring change as we come into agreement with it. Engaging Transformation may reveal and open up for you the transformation you need to experience. Engage Refiner's Fire and a portal opens up to the fire of God. But do not be limited by what I have described here, because each of them can have different connotations. And then they all interact. For example, if you stand between Winds of Change and Transformation it will perhaps open up a portal for you to engage in a new season of deeper transformation in your life.

Do try this at home!

You can create this in your own quiet place, your own secret place with God, your own living room. You can picture this and engage it, and continue engaging it so that a portal will open when you stand in your living room between two angels or two faces. Let me say again, this is not just for us in a local *ekklesia* in a small town in the southwest of England, this is a representation of what God wants to do everywhere. Perhaps we are forerunners, but forerunners open up something for everyone. We may do this in our own peculiar way with flags and banners but you can do it spiritually even if you do not have flags and banners. You can picture it in your imagination and say "I'm inviting the four angels of transformation to come. I'm inviting the four living creatures to bring heaven and earth into agreement and I'm going to step into it." You can do that every day, if you want to, until you have gone into all the different portals between all the different arcs. You will find it transports you to places you never knew were there.

And He said to him, "Truly, truly, I say to you, you will see the heavens opened and the angels of God ascending and descending on the Son of Man" (John 1:51).

Jesus was drawing their attention to the reality of a great deal of spiritual activity around His life. If we are to be like Him, we need that kind of spiritual activity around our life too. The rivers of living water flowing from within us will create an atmosphere around us which draws and welcomes the angelic realm. When they sense it around you, the living creatures and the men in white linen are attracted by an atmosphere of heaven on the earth. And if you, as a gateway of heaven, let the flow of living water create even a small bubble of that atmosphere around your life, heaven will begin to manifest around you on the earth.

Jesus described Himself as living in dual realms of earth and heaven when speaking to Nicodemus:

No one has ascended to heaven but He who came down from heaven, that is, the Son of Man who is in heaven (John 3:13 NKJV).

So we can live in both of these realms; and we can learn to be in the four faces of God and be a gateway for that to manifest on the earth all the time: not just stepping into heaven and stepping back out but living in and living out. We want to live in the manifest presence and live out the manifest presence of God. That is actually one of our visionary statements, it is something we want to teach and enable people to do.

This may be new to you, but it is real. We can engage it and discover a whole different level of authority and government in it as God wants us to engage and experience these things. So I want to encourage you to just have a go at this. I could carry on explaining all my experiences but you need to have your own.

Activation #11: Engage arcs and portals

Engage with Transformation, Winds of Change, Sound of Many Waters and Refiner's Fire. Engage in the arcs between them: just stand in the middle and see what opens up, see what you experience. Angels are ministering spirits on our behalf: they are here to help.

What change do you want in your life? What new season do you want to come into? If you want to change, go and ask Transformation whether there is something you need to come into agreement with the will of God about. If you do not know the will of God, go and engage the Sound of Many

Waters, the voice of His presence. And as you go on, all these things will start to connect up for you.

Transformation: we can be transformed into the image of Jesus. Our behaviour can be changed; our thinking can be changed. We can be transfigured to shine with glory. We need to open our heart and respond to the revelation that we receive from Transformation.

Winds of Change: we can enter into a new season of sonship, a new season of blessing: joy, peace, authority and power as a son to change and transform circumstances around our life by ruling, overcoming and subduing. Open your heart and breathe the breath of life that comes as the wind blows.

Refiner's Fire: Seraphim. Greater passion for God, for our life and destiny. A pure heart to see God. Our life can be purified and refined as we engage. Any chains restricting us can be burned away, consumed, so that we are free. Open your heart for that passion, purification, destroying of chains – or for whatever happens as you engage.

Sound of Many Waters: the vibrational frequency of the voice of God. Everything that is not of God's kingdom can be shaken from us when we start to vibrate and resonate with the frequency of God's voice. If we are carrying a lower frequency and we engage with His higher frequency, it will raise our frequency and bring us back into alignment with His call, with His voice. Resonate with the truth of your identity as a son and let that frequency raise up your expectations; let Him speak His word of affirmation, calling you into sonship. Our whole body can be aligned with that frequency to bring health and wholeness. Our DNA can be transformed by the Sound of Many Waters. Open your heart to that frequency in God's voice.

Be willing to engage all these arcs and portals. Take a moment of reflection and then go where you feel led to go. And as I did, you can keep coming back to experience different arcs and portals each time.

169

Note: this is an unstructured activation so there is no text or guided voice audio for it. However, please do not skip over it or omit it altogether. You can refer to the diagrams of flags and banners in chapter 4 (or the colour versions on the resources page) if they help. We also suggest some suitable background music on the resources page, but feel free to use whatever music helps you engage. If you have access to essential oils or other natural fragrances, you may wish to diffuse those too.

13. Engage in Eternity

Restored connection

As sons of God we have access to I AM, and to what was before there was anything other than God, when we were just a twinkle in His eye and a thought in His heart. We can now engage with that again: the eternal aspects of our identity and destiny, outside of time and space.

We were doing things before we came here, and we can reconnect to that because it gives us inspiration at a spiritual level to inform and empower what we do here. God assigned us to creation before we came here physically, so we were involved in creation as sons but we have forgotten that. God wants to restore our connection, both to creation and to His heart.

God never panics. How could He panic when it is all 'now'? But people have different views of time: some believe that the future is already there, fixed, and in time it will just happen; but in that case what involvement would we have in it? I do not believe the future is fixed; I believe that God's heart in eternity holds His desire for what will be, and that we are responsible for partnering with Him in creating what will be.

As I saw within the mind of God, every single person who has ever existed and ever will exist are within the 'now' of His eternal state. Every one of us is making decisions and choices every millisecond of our lives and He is connected to every one of them in that instant. When I first engaged that, it was just overwhelming, but it showed me His heart and His love for everybody and for creation itself. He is constantly making course corrections to help us get some good out of the sometimes foolish decisions we make and to bring us back on course.

Nothing is ever a surprise for Him. He is never fazed and He already planned, before everything even started, to make sure that we would be restored to face-to-face, blameless innocence in relationship. Jesus was the Lamb slain before the foundation of the world.

As we begin to engage in His heart of love for everyone and everything, it motivates us to find the part we have to play, to reconnect to our assignment in creation. Sometimes people just know in their heart that there is something that they are stirred to, and they do not know why. When we do get to know why, and that God has assigned us to a certain area as a son of God, as a created light being, then it starts to empower us in what we are doing here. And then in the ages to come we have an ongoing destiny to be outworked as we go forward as sons of God.

It is an important place to engage. I like to think of it as our eternal home in the dance of God's love. When I am there, it is full of life and energy. I begin to connect up to the sum of His thoughts of me and I hear snatches of conversation about me. When I first went there, I could not go with my mind because it was nonlinear, and I was not able to be nonlinear at that point, until I got deconstructed and renewed. I can now connect up in a different way, though it is still way beyond what I can fathom or describe. But I find I just know things instinctively because I am part of the thoughts of God, His heart and His desire. As I absorb that revelation, it then begins to direct my life: I begin to be active in a particular sphere or have a desire to get involved in certain things which I never would have done if I had not connected to them there.

We can all be in that marvellous place of God's love, in relationship with Him and in that wonderful dance. That is where true intimacy and true identity come from: a restored relationship with the very essence of God, the very essence of love. And that is not just feeling loved, which is wonderful in itself, but being able to be an expression of love ourselves (even if that is a work in progress).

None of us are perfect yet, and some areas of our lives may be awesome and other areas feel like a train wreck. We may be mature in some ways and childish or damaged in others.

But if we are in a process, God will look to help deal with the train wreck because He works in us continually. He does not say "Until you deal with your train wreck, you can't be here." So He is working with us to restore us, not just to experience love but to be an expression of love and to love creation.

Living loved, loving living and then living loving really is what God's desire is for us, because that is what He is like. He takes pleasure and joy in everything He has created, including us. When He looks at us, it brings Him such pleasure! We are the apple of His eye; we are the treasure of His heart.

Our spiritual memory can be restored, but it may take some deconstruction before that becomes cognitive. I needed a lot of deconstruction, as I have shared elsewhere, to get rid of my mindsets and my framework of religious (and other) thinking so that my spiritual memory became remapped over my mind, over my consciousness.

I got deconstructed over several years, and then I started to get renewed, and to remember what I was doing before I was here. I began to be reconnected, and my mind started to operate nonlinearly, from the perspective of the creative light of God. Once our soul and spirit have been separated and reintegrated, our spirit can then move and direct us while our soul agrees and cooperates. When the soul and spirit are separated, it deals with the ego, my soul needing affirmation in the wrong way (to affirm its own identity independent of God). When my soul and spirit became reintegrated and came into agreement and wholeness, it changed everything for me. I believe everyone needs to go through that process[7], though the details may be different for everyone, because it will get you to the point where soul and spirit are in agreement and you can live in heaven and on earth at the same time.

---

[7] We describe separating soul and spirit in two blog posts on freedomarc.blog

173

We can then become reconnected with who we were as pre-existing spirit beings, and reconnected to creation as it was before it came into the bondage of corruption. Having that memory of what it was like when it was in perfect harmony and there was no darkness really motivates me to want to see it that way again. It is groaning and in bondage, waiting for the sons of God to be revealed to bring it into freedom, the freedom of the glory of the children of God.

Walk the ancient path

We have seen this diagram before, the figure of eight 'infinity' symbol which is what I see as the eternal circle. We can stand in 'what is' every day, in heaven, in the arc of the name of God, in His name, in the four faces of God; and then we have access to walk on that ancient path back into the heart of God.

For me, now, I do not walk back into it because I just reside there. And I also reside in the middle and try to walk out what I am flowing from there (with greater or lesser success). When things do not go well, it may be because I have made choices which were not too smart. Why did I make those choices? Most likely I was listening to the wrong thoughts. Sometimes that happens, but the more we spend time and are consciously aware of being in His heart, the more His heart has an opportunity of creating those desires in our heart which will cause us to work it out and walk it out every day.

We are in the midst of a process of cosmic transformation so everything is not yet as it will be. Some parts are still broken: it does not all work as God intends. Sometimes we may come across what seems like a great many of those broken parts: then we have to make sure we are not affected by them and that we bring change and restoration into them.

It is an interesting walk! I know that I am in multiple places and my being in all of them contributes to what I am doing here; but so far I can still only really cognitively engage one place at a time. If I focus on being seated on my throne in the realm of heaven, then I only have to shift my consciousness from this realm and I am there, and I can describe to you what is going on there. But then to describe to you where I am in the heart of God in eternity I would have to stop thinking about my throne and start thinking about the heart of God in eternity instead. Eventually we may be able to connect to all those thoughts cognitively, but for now the process of inhabiting those different realms is still rewiring, remapping and reconfiguring my consciousness to be able to operate as a son of God.

In this process, you can only start where you are. So you may be just beginning to focus on being in the name of God and in the four faces of God. If so, you can walk this eternal circle, as they did to make covenant. The blood was in the middle, where the paths cross: they would walk around and meet in the middle to confirm their agreement and then they would live that agreement out in their lives. We are in the New Covenant, with open access to God without going through any mediator: we have access to be in the name of God, access to be in His heart, and we can then begin to flow from that.

It is a process, not an event, and it is a process in which we need one another. Let's say you are engaging the mind of God, which is so vast that you are only going to get a glimpse of the part that refers to you, and your destiny. Others will connect up with their part, their destiny; and when we put it all together, we get something greater than the sum of the parts.

175

We cannot act as if we are independent individuals within the Mountain of the House of the Lord, it is corporate. We are living stones within a larger whole, although each of us is still a house of God ourselves. Everything with God works as a fractal. If you are not familiar with fractals, look at the frond of a fern: it looks just like the whole fern! Look deeper, and the mini-fronds on the mini-ferns all look just like the fern too. That is how heaven operates. Each of us is part of the bigger picture and we are all part of the fractal whole that is God Himself.

In His heart in eternity you can rest and allow His thoughts to envelop you. It is like being in the womb of His heart: you were birthed there and you can feel His love, you can feel His frequency vibrating in your spirit and then revealed from your spirit to your heart. All those amazing thoughts about you: if He were to tell you all of them in one go you would never be able to take it in, so He gives you what you need, bit by bit. It builds you up and nourishes you and nurtures you so that you begin to become more aware of your sonship. Most people, if they know it at all, only know their sonship in relation to this realm. We can know who we were as a son and who we will be as a son, though for now we are in the middle. We can connect up the beginning to the end in agreement, because we are in the middle and walking it out.

So we can listen to Him unveil the hidden mysteries of our destiny. So many people just want to see their scroll and read it all. God will not let us read it all: first, because we would think it was impossible; and second, because we would try to figure out how to do it, rather than just 'being'. He reveals what we need to know on a day to day basis; that is why we have to walk with Him in relationship every day. Then every day we will find new mercies for that day. We only get what we need for today. We do not yet have what we will need for tomorrow; we will get that tomorrow. And yesterday's is gone, so if we are still thinking about what we should have been doing yesterday, we are using up today's resources by worrying about what we did not do; and if we keep thinking about what we might have to do tomorrow, we will use up today's resources by worrying about tomorrow. Jesus told us that today has enough of its own to think about. As we seek first the kingdom, everything we need will be given to us.

I know we sometimes have to make decisions which affect our future, but that can come out of knowing the love of God today: the peace we have today can help us make decisions for what we need to do tomorrow. That place of peace and rest enables us to carry the heart of God for what we might need to do in the future without having to worry about it or fret about it. We only have to take a step at a time, day by day.

Identity and purpose

In this place of intimacy He will reveal how special you are to Him. You will begin to feel your value and worth to Him, not because of what you can do but because of who you are: His child. Our own children all have characteristics that are different but we love them all the same. Let's say one of our children has a fantastic university degree and another one never really performed well academically, that would not affect how much we love them (at least, we would hope not). They would be of equal value to us. God loves and values us all the same, regardless of what we may have done or failed to do. His love is unconditional.[8] Society may value certain individuals more than others, but God does not. He does not value us according to what we can do for Him: we are His children so He will reveal our true identity; and our purpose which derives from that identity, not the other way around.

So many people are searching to find their identity in their purpose, which means that if they stop 'doing', they feel like they no longer know who they are. As soon as God removes something from them they fall apart because they do not know who they are. We have seasons in which we are called

---

[8] Explore *Unconditional Love* in the free video series at eg.freedomarc.org/love

to do certain things, just like in a family when you have young children you have to do things very differently from when they grow up and flee the nest. If my children have left home, who am I now? I am still a parent, and they are still my children, although our roles have changed significantly within that relationship. But I am still me, and my identity does not depend on what I do.

The Father wants us all to know our identity and our purpose. Then let us be transformed to release what we will be. When we know God's heart, it enables us to say "I want to be like that." If I am not yet like that, then I am transforming, resonating with my destiny because we are in relationship. I do not allow my destiny to become my primary concern: my primary concern is relationship. Destiny will automatically begin to outwork because we are in relationship.

Scrolls

When you engage scrolls of revelation and destiny in this place, they are more like thoughts than a list of instructions or directives. Do not necessarily expect to see a large number of scrolls and to read them all. A scroll is just something that contains information, a revelation, a truth, a mandate or whatever it might be. The scroll in itself is nothing: it is what it conveys that is the important thing.

So when you are looking to engage in God's heart, expect it to be like thoughts in your mind or feelings in your heart, not just to be information that you can read. At one time I used to desperately need to know everything; I was wired that way. Once I was freed from needing to know everything, God was free to show me everything He wanted to show me. We do not need to read every scroll. God reveals to us what we need, and not necessarily by reading. He wants us to receive the revelation by whatever means is suitable for us, and for it to begin to draw, shape and move us in the direction He intends.

For example, my scroll has my governmental position encoded within it, with the nine attributes of government

178

revealed in God's precepts, statutes, laws, ordinances, mantles, weapons, scrolls, discoveries, commissioning into sonship etc. My scroll enables me to recognise and resonate with all things that are part of my destiny: including relationship, tasks, quests, trials, mandates, ministry positions and callings.

Our scrolls may reveal who we were in eternity past, our true identity, our redemptive gift[9], our purpose, our destiny; what we will be and what we will do. But remember, we are human beings not human doings, who will become spirit beings and godlike beings: it is always about being, not doing. The doing will flow from the being, as long as we are at peace and do not strive. So do not focus too much on what your future governmental role may be, because then you will risk missing out on what you could be doing now. Be at rest. That governmental position will come about for you as you walk out your relationship.

There are two natural DNA strands in our physical body and they carry the record of our mother and father and our generational line. There is a third strand, a light strand, which carries the record of our eternal image and purpose. When we realise who we are, that third strand starts to express the characteristics of the light that we carry as the sons of God. This is why our DNA needs to be transformed: we are no longer children of Adam, we are now new creations in Christ; so our physical DNA needs to be transformed to come into agreement with the new creation.

My destiny scroll has a preface or overview, a blueprint that aligns my life and directs the desires of my heart. My scroll is encoded in light that begins to release desire into my heart

---

[9] *Destiny Redemptive Gifts* is a 4-part audio series available either as a standalone on our website or as part of an *Engaging God* subscription. It also makes up a series of 7 blog posts at freedomarc.blog

and transform and conform me to my eternal image. My scroll is opened day by day to direct my paths.

Your word is a lamp to my feet
And a light to my path (Psalm 119:105).

For the word of God is living and active, and sharper than any two-edged sword, even penetrating as far as the division of soul and spirit, of both joints and marrow, and able to judge the thoughts and intentions of the heart (Hebrews 4:12).

Neither of those familiar verses are talking about 'the Bible', by the way, but about the living word that God spoke in eternity, which is active in me.

All through relationship

There is no manual for this: it is all through relationship. I can actively engage my scroll in many places, including the scroll room, the Arc, and here, in God's heart in eternity; but it is better to pursue relationship. I used to go and try to find my scroll every day. I would go and say, "What is Your will and purpose for me today? I surrender my will. I want to be a living sacrifice: I present myself to You. I want to fulfil my destiny. I want You to tell me what to do." I was wanting a to-do list: do this today, don't do that.

Therefore Jesus answered and was saying to them, "Truly, truly, I say to you, the Son can do nothing of Himself, unless it is something He sees the Father doing; for whatever the Father does, these things the Son also does in the same way" (John 5:19).

Jesus only did what He saw the Father doing. He did not have a list. It was not that He was reading a scroll (or watching a heavenly video) with the minutest detail of every miracle He was going to do that day recorded on it: He did not get "Heal 15 blind people today, and do it such and such a way for each one." He had the heart of the Father to heal people, to restore their sight, and He did it in all kinds of creative ways. When

180

we have that kind of relationship, that state of being releases a flow of everything we do.

God showed me that when I first engaged the arc, I was engaging with what was in the arc and not the four faces of God. As I said, I never saw them. I was looking into the arc and I saw the manna, representing the will of God. I wanted His will, and He honoured that. But then when He took it to another level and I went into the four faces, all of a sudden I did not need a list, I had His heart.

There is no formula in relationship, as Christianity or any other religion likes to have, all neatly packaged into a nice tidy theological system. "We know how God works, and it is like this. Just obey this set of rules." In that case we have just swapped out one set of rules for another, the laws of the Old Covenant for a new set of rules in the New Covenant.

In reality, there are no rules for us, just relationship. God wants to move us in our hearts because we know His heart; and then as sons we get to outwork that relationship. It is wonderful, it frees you up no end because you can just be. And the more connected you are to His heart, when you are living in that realm, the more that is flowing through you here.

So many Christians I know feel guilty when they are not doing anything. But God likes to rest: and we can live in rest. We do not need always to be thinking, "What should I be doing now? Should I be doing something? And am I going to get it wrong?" There is no 'should': it is a word I am trying to remove from my vocabulary. We can be at complete rest, knowing that God loves us and if we do make some poor decisions then He can work good out of them, bring us back to Him again and restore us. That is what He is doing all the time, continually at work in our lives to help us walk out the path.

Through your scroll you may get a sense of your overall purpose, but that will only come because you are connecting with God in relationship. As you engage God, you take on His DNA and become joined to Him:

181

But the one who joins himself to the Lord is one spirit with Him (1 Corinthians 6:17).

As we grow into maturity, we can behold and become conformed to that image. Keep looking at His face, keep breathing in His life; behold and become. This happens as we step into Him, as we are baptised in Him, as we stand on the fire stones, as we dance with Him on the dance floor, as we are skinned with His nature and character and armour, and as we engage His heart in eternity. All these things contribute to our growing in maturity and conforming to His image.

Questions of destiny

Some of the questions people ask when we start to talk about destiny are:

- 'Who am I?'
- 'Where do I come from?'
- 'Who created me?'
- 'Why and how did He create me?'

These are good questions, but God does not want to just answer them, nor does He want us to try to figure them out for ourselves. He wants us to have a relationship with Him in which those answers are revealed to us. And that can begin right where we are in our relationship with Him.

God is eternal. He has always been, He is, and He will always be (see Revelation 1:8). He is almighty, that is 'all-mighty'. He is light (1 John 1:5). He is love (1 John 4:16). He is spirit (John 4:24). And the Bible will tell you hundreds more names of God. He is called our high tower, our shield, our deliverer, our Saviour, our healer, our righteousness, our sanctification, our banner, our Shepherd and many more. Name upon name, but they are just words on a page unless you have experienced Him as your Shepherd, banner, healer or all-mighty.

We need to explore and experience, so if we meditate on those scriptures and others like them they begin to open up a door for us to engage who God is. Before I was meeting Him

182

face to face all the time, I would meditate on scriptures and they would just begin to unfold something: thoughts would come into my mind and I would begin to connect to them.

That is a good place to start, if you are reading this thinking "Going into eternity? Can I do that? How would anyone even know how to do that?" Start with where you are, and journey towards where you will be. I did not go into eternity on day one, it took me many years of walking this journey to find that I had access to something I never dreamed possible. If someone had told me I could go outside of time and space and go into the heart of God I would have wondered whatever they were talking about. As maybe you are now. But when I had the experience, then I knew. So if we engage Him and get to know Him, wherever we are now, our intimate relationship with Him will help us know who we are through this face-to-face beholding experience.

This is what God said of Jeremiah:

"Before I formed you in the womb I knew you,
And before you were born I consecrated you;
I have appointed you as a prophet to the nations" (Jeremiah 1:5).

And when we are looking at who God made us to be, all of us were formed in His heart before we were formed in the womb. All of us are consecrated and all of us are appointed to something. And in the intimacy of our relationship with God, we can hear Him calling our name. As I have described, I saw my name written on my throne in heaven when I first went there in 2008, and I resonated with that name which was a description of me as God sees me. Now when I hear that name in heaven it draws me, my ears prick up in the spirit, and I have found that it happens a lot if we are willing to listen.

We are not some vague thought that God had but a very specific one. We existed before we were in the womb. God has always known us, from His perspective, and since intimacy is two-way, actually we knew Him too. Although we did not come into this world with the full memory of everything, some of it draws us; it is encoded within us but we have to discover it again.

So what is the name He has given you? I encourage you to ask Him if you do not know what it is. Your name will also begin to reveal your identity; and that will release you into what you are appointed to be (and do). I would not start with "What am I appointed to do?" without first knowing your identity and your name. I would not ask Him to show you your scroll, but to unveil your identity, revealing what flows out from that identity.

The image of the heavenly

As is the earthy, so also are those who are earthy; and as is the heavenly, so also are those who are heavenly. Just as we have borne the image of the earthy, we will also bear the image of the heavenly (1 Corinthians 15:48-49).

We need the earthly and the heavenly to be working together. We already have a heavenly image, which needs to be outworked through what we do here. They are not separate, but complementary. We were born with this earthly body but we are also born from above: our spirit is active and alive to God, so we can bear that heavenly image on the earth. How do we get to the point where we can do that consistently? Through rest, through relationship, through intimacy.

We are in a place where we can begin to experience far more than we ever imagined or thought possible. God is opening up the door for us to engage with the heavenly realms, so that we can both see and reflect what is going on.

How precious also are Your thoughts to me, O God!
How vast is the sum of them! (Psalm 139:17).

God wants us to know those thoughts, to get hold of those thoughts and let them transform us. I guarantee not one of us knows one hundred percent of the way God thinks about us! But little by little we can listen and hear; and the more we allow God's thoughts towards us to affect the way we think about ourselves, the more transformation takes place and the more our lives become like Jesus. He is the Son of God; we are sons of God. The more we are conformed to His image, the more we will do the things He did (and greater things, as He promised). Many of us have been trying to do the things He did without having the image of sonship, so it has become formulaic. We have tried to learn how to minister to people, how to heal people. We have tried to learn techniques; really we just need to be sons, then we will be able to do the things that sons do.

The thoughts of God towards us today are totally in tune with what was written on our scroll before the foundation of the world. I have heard people teach that our scroll contains all the bad things that have happened to us: it does not. And some of them are angry with God because He put all those terrible things on their scroll. There is nothing bad on your scroll; but we live in a fallen, broken environment that is not yet fully restored, and things happen to us that are not as God intended. Yes, He can even use those things to bring good and weave them into His story, but it does not mean that when we agreed our scroll, we agreed that those bad things would happen to us. Destiny is not fate. We have a choice to agree with God to pursue it or not.

Activation #12: Engage eternity

I want to open up the opportunity for you to walk back into eternity and to re-engage with the eternal aspect of the heart of God there. Again, I cannot guarantee that you will be able to do that; I did not do it right at the beginning of my journey. But ask the Father or ask Jesus to take you if you are ready; or if not, to take you wherever is right for you. Wherever He takes you will be part of your journey into that realm.

Read the text first and then close your eyes and engage. Or you can listen to the audio, either from the resources page or by scanning the QR code.

185

Heaven is open.
Close your eyes and think of that open heaven.

Allow a picture of the open heaven to form,
and the ladder leading up there.
Hear the invitation to 'come up here.'
Engage with Jesus, who is standing in the door.

And as you step into that realm
ask Jesus to help you engage
with the Arc within the tabernacle
because that's where we are going to go
to access eternity.

Let Jesus lead you first of all
to the Arc of the presence of God.
And we can stand in the Arc of the presence of God
within the four faces.
Seeing the four faces,
within the *Yod Hei Vav Hei* of His name;
the four faces of the lion, ox, eagle and man.

So we can stand before the four faces
and then step into His name.

That is a step of choice,
to step into the manifestation of His presence there.
As you step into His presence,
ask Jesus to allow you to walk on the ancient paths
to engage in His heart.

Then you may find yourself transported into that place,
or you may find Jesus will walk with you there.
Just step with Him and walk in,
wherever He leads you,
wherever you go.

When you are there,
within the heart of God's presence,
you may feel cocooned in love
you may feel the Father revealing

that deep sense of His love for you,
revealing His heart for you.

You may see yourself as a light being,
a being of light.

You may be aware of the conversation all around you.
You may hear His thoughts about you.
You may feel who you were always meant to be,
sense your eternal identity.

Who knows what it will be?

But I encourage you now to relax
and allow that to take place.
Allow Him to take you back into that place of intimacy,
that place of awesome relationship,
where the eternal aspect of who you are
will begin to be unveiled to you
at a deeper and deeper level.

Stay there as long as you want or need to.

Let me remind you once again not to allow any of these little exercises to be a one-time experience. Return to them over and over until you develop heavenly engagement as a lifestyle. You are never going to receive all He wants to release to you in one experience, however intense it may be. Engage over and over again, going deeper and deeper, so that the revelation of who you are will arise from the revelation of who He is.

14. The Court of the Lord

Destiny revealed

The Court of the Lord is another place we can engage in the realms of heaven, where our scroll and our destiny were agreed before we came to the earth. We were in relationship with God in an eternal sense, but how did we get here? How did we transition from where we were to where we now are?

It seems as if we suddenly appeared here when we were conceived in our mother's womb. I believe that in eternity we were sons of God, sons of light: light beings made in the image of God, functioning in that realm and having connection to creation itself. We then agreed to come into this realm – it was not forced upon us – and our scroll was revealed to us, describing our earthly destiny and all we are called to do here and into the ages to come.

As we saw, we did not agree to anything harmful, but to God's intention and desire for us. We came into agreement and cooperation with that then; so if we are to agree with Him now, we really need to rediscover our destiny (His intention and desire for us) again. When we come into this physical realm, we do not have the memory of connection; so although God has never separated Himself from us, we think we are separated, and therefore we live separated.

For as he thinks in his heart, so is he (Proverbs 23:7a NKJV).

People may believe and live according to all sorts of different ways of thinking. If you believe that you are a sinner, you are likely to live like a sinner; but if you believe that you are a son of God then you can live like a son of God. Of course, you have to know what being a son of God means: by now you realise that it is all about relationship and an unveiling of our full identity within that relationship. So if we choose to agree now, it is essential for us to get hold of His thoughts towards us and progressively get to know what is written on our scroll.

Even though there is something about it that guides us from within, even before we recognise it cognitively, we are called to actively participate in it. God does not want us to know only His works, and to try to do the works of God, but also to get to know His ways, which only comes by revelation. And He wants us to be involved in the various courts, councils and assemblies which comprise the decision-making processes of heaven. One of those courts is the Court of the Lord, the *Sod* of God, to which we have access.

I first went there when I wanted to look at my scroll because 'I needed to know' what was on it. I wanted to be able to do everything that was on my scroll, so I produced a *ketubah*, which included all my expectations of what I was going to be able to do to fulfil my destiny. I really did want to fulfil my destiny, but I had mixed motives and some of them were coming out of my soul: my soul needed to know, rather than resting in relationship and trusting God.

So I would counsel you not to seek for your scroll so that you can feel safe and secure in knowing what is on it; instead seek God, seek the relationship, and see what comes out of that. Yes, we can engage the scroll room in heaven, where the scribes are. I went there looking for my scroll one day and I could not find it! I was looking for it by my date of birth and then one of the scribes took me and showed me that the date of my physical birth was not when I reconnected to my scroll, it was when I first rediscovered who I was as a son of God. I did not know when that was: he showed me that was in September 1970, but I was still not allowed to see my scroll at that time.

Opening my scroll

Eventually, though, that did happen. It was the very first time I had sat on the Father's lap on the Throne of Grace. I had an amazing encounter, feeling so at peace, so at rest, and so loved. Then the Spirit of the Fear of the Lord came, the one of the seven spirits of God I had never met before, and he brought my scroll. The Father said to take it, and I thought,

189

"Great! I'm going to be able to look at it!" Then the Spirit of the Fear of the Lord led me to what looked like the mouth of the lion and I knew that I had to go in there. So I took my scroll and stepped in – it was like going into a huge, dark cave. This was very early in my experiences in heaven and I was really scared. I had no idea what was waiting for me in there. Still, I walked in. I kept going until I came to the fire of God's presence. And from the fire of God's presence, the fire of His eyes penetrated me. Thankfully, I knew that I was loved because I had just been sitting on the Father's lap, but I was also apprehensive about what was going to happen.

The scroll was sealed front and back, so I did not know how to open it. Then I remembered the scripture about who is worthy to open the scroll, so I presented it to Him. As I did, the seals flew off and it opened in front of me. My whole life flashed before my eyes – at least, everything concerning my relationship with God and everything I had done as His son. To start with, He showed me all the gold, silver and precious stones which represented all the times when I had responded in relationship, love and obedience, and I felt the pleasure of His heart. It was just beautiful.

His eyes were burning into me, and I was really glad He had chosen to do it in that order, because then there was all the wood, hay and stubble, all that God wanted me to do but that I had done for my own sake or with mixed motives, because it made me feel good, gave me a position or accorded me some sort of recognition. That was not so good. But the fire of God's love just consumed it all from my scroll; I sensed that it was redeeming everything and restoring my ability to reconnect to everything in a more relational way.

I was not going to turn my back on Him, so I carefully backed out, only to find the Spirit of the Fear of the Lord looking intently at me. For a moment, I wondered why. And then I realised there was another side to the scroll: I needed to go back in, and it might as well be now.

190

So I did, and again the seals came off and the other side of my scroll was revealed. It was filled with all the missed opportunities God had given me which I just never saw. I felt sorrow and regret, but no condemnation or guilt, just sadness that I had missed so much because I was not listening, or got distracted or was thinking about doing something else. Again, that all got consumed.

When they read in the Bible about going before the judgment seat of Christ, most people think that only happens after you die. It is not: you can go now. You can experience it as an ongoing refining, making sure that your scroll is filled with the things that are producing gold, silver and precious stones.

Our scroll is something that we can engage in, and it is an ongoing process. Someone once asked me if their scroll could be changed. It can, and constantly, because God is constantly outworking things to ensure that anything we have done can be redeemed. We connect to our scroll to ensure that our destiny is continually being revealed, unveiled, outworked and fulfilled.

Ya Sod

As well as in the scroll room, we can engage our destiny on the fire stones, absorbing revelation of our sonship and who we are; and we can engage the heart of God in eternity, in that womb where we were formed, being cocooned in the love of God, and again have a revelation of when we went under the Shepherd's rod[10] to agree our scroll.

That is also where our angels were assigned to us for the outworking of our destiny: they are here as ministering spirits on our behalf to help us fulfil our destiny. We can engage with the vast sum of His thoughts about us and begin to perceive

---

[10] From Psalm 23 we see that the shepherd's rod is for protection and security, not for beating us with!

and have a more cognitive experience, though the details only need to come when you need to know them.

But you can also engage the Court of the Lord, the *Ya Sod* of God. I believe we all engaged that court or council when we became a living soul; when we were assigned our destiny, our scroll was revealed, our angels were assigned to us and we were commissioned into sonship in this dimension. As we mature in sonship we can access the *Sod* again, but in a different capacity, as part of God's council, to be involved in its discussions as He is outworking things today.

That realm is still a created realm and it still functions in time, though a different time scale than ours; and we can engage it there to ensure that God's purposes are being outworked. Many people are afraid of what might happen in the future, whether World War III or an asteroid impact that wipes out life on the planet. Those things are not God's intention, and they will not happen because that is what these councils determine. We are not just subject to chance. There may be other destructive forces in play, but the councils of God set limits on what can and cannot happen; and as we engage the courts of God as sons, we start to decree, declare and legislate for God's purposes to be outworked.

From that perspective we start to see the enemy's plans and can thwart them before they even begin. A few years ago, just before Christmas, our regional Bench of Three engaged heaven and we were given some insight into a terrorist plot being planned for Christmas in the UK. We determined, not on our watch. We went into the mobile court and asked for the accusations to be brought that might enable it to go ahead. There were a considerable number of them, but we stood in identification with our nation for people and we took the accusations, agreed with them and got a verdict. Then we used that verdict to decree peace over the Christmas period.

Nothing happened. Some might argue that nothing was going to happen anyway, that it was just coincidence, but we know what we did and we know what we heard. You may object that sometimes such things do happen. In those cases, maybe there was no one to legislate, or they did not when they could have. Or perhaps they did not hear or were not listening. I do not know.

I do know that there are councils and assemblies and courts in heaven such as the Council of the Lord overseeing this, and also the Council of Judges and the Council of Seventy. On some councils, many of the places are not occupied by the people they are intended for, so they are occupied by angels or by men in white linen, some of the ancient ones and others. More of us are beginning to be involved because we have discovered that we have access to stand in the councils and assemblies of God, but we are only able to do so as we go through the process of maturing and coming into government.

Bible scholar Patrick Miller has said that "one of the central cosmological symbols of the Old Testament is the imagery of the divine council."[11] We know that the Old Testament is full of images and symbols, including the Hebrew letters (which are living beings), but they can be quite difficult for us to understand if we have not been brought up in that culture. But here is an expert who has looked at biblical symbolism and realised that the Old Testament is filled with the imagery of courts and councils, though we may only see the more obvious ones. God has an entourage of the angelic realm and many others who have functions within the kingdom to outwork His will. Principalities and powers, rulers and thrones were created for government and for us to work with. If you look at the Bible, angels were involved in many aspects of Jesus' life and the lives of many other individuals.

Another scholar, Paul Sumner, defines the Council or *Sod* of God as "a symbolic ruling body consisting of God as the

[11] Patrick D. Miller, Israelite Religion and Biblical Theology: Collected Essays (vol. 267; Journal for the Study of the Old Testament Supplement Series; Sheffield: Sheffield Academic Press, 2000).

supreme monarch with an assembly of supernatural servants gathered around His throne in a heavenly palace."[12]

The word 'symbolic' does not mean that it is not real. It is just that the reality of something which exists in a spiritual realm is often presented to us in a symbolic way to help us connect to it. Remember, the Greek language is all about form, what it looks like; but the Hebrew is more about function, what it does. If we focus on what it looks like, we can miss the point of what is going on there. The metaphorical imagery depicts actual realities in the divine world in a way we can relate to.

YHVH is king. He works with His divine servants to outwork His will but He does not want only servants, but sons. The angels are His sons in one sense but they do not carry His DNA as we do. He wants us as sons to be involved in the family business, in all kinds of different ways: one of which is in the boardroom, if you like, at the heart of the decision-making and the executive. God has chosen not just to act sovereignly: He sets out the intent and purpose and everyone on the board can have their say about how to make it happen. If it is not relational, it is not God.

Israel knew about this heavenly council because Joshua the High Priest, Ezekiel and others encountered it. We call these 'throne visions,' first-hand reports of a 'divine council' or 'divine assembly' in session, and they are in the Bible. That is important to some people, but there is so much more that is not in the Bible than is; and just because it is not in the Bible specifically does not mean it is not real or not true. Perhaps a better question to ask about something unfamiliar to us is 'Does it align with what we know of God's nature and character? Does it align with love?' If it contradicts love, it is not God.

---

[12] Paul Sumner: Visions of the Heavenly Council in the Hebrew Bible. hebrew-streams.org

God takes His position in His assembly;
He judges in the midst of the gods (Psalm 82:1).

Elohim standeth in the Adat El;
He judgeth among the elohim (Psalm 82:1 OJB).

There you have God, called *Elohim*, and others who are also called *elohim*. Some of our English versions translate this as 'God' and 'gods.' There is one God, but these others are described as *elohim* because they are like God, they are the sons of God. If we are to sit in that assembly then we need to learn to do things like God; and only in relationship with Him will we be able to understand and take on His nature and character. We need to act like Him, think like Him, respond like Him, and love like Him.

If you get involved in governmental things in heaven with a wrong view of God, you can be quite judgmental. I have heard of people doing things, supposedly in the courts of heaven, which are just outrageous because they are not representing God at all (and I cannot believe that they are really in a heavenly court, because no heavenly judge would permit bringing retribution upon people). If we deal with people in a heavenly court, we forgive them and bless them, we do not curse them or try to get revenge or payback.

Council gatherings

There are three terms used for council gatherings in the Old Testament: *edah*, *qahal*, and *sod*.

Edah means congregation, assembly, or company. It is also used for the congregation of Israel.

Qahal refers to gathering together, and parallels the later Greek words *synagogue* and *ekklesia*.

Sod designates a king's inner circle, his closest friends and counsellors who know his mind and discuss his plans. To participate in the *sod* is a profound privilege. It is something

195

like a Privy Council, and some members of YHWH's *sod* are referred to in scripture as Chancellors or High Chancellors.

All three words indicate ways in which the patterns of heaven get outworked on the earth. That is the purpose of them all, to bring earth back to its redeemed, reconciled and restored place within the creation order. Originally earth and heaven were together: our physical realm was completely connected to the spiritual realm. Then it fell from that estate, through various falls to where we are now. Creation is crying out to be restored back to that state; and for that to happen we need to be there first.

When we get restored to these positions of government then we can begin to legislate and make decrees, declarations and agreements within this purpose, for the whole of creation to be restored. And God is not sitting there telling people what to do; quite often He says "Well, who will go for us?" – looking for volunteers and those who will cooperate with His purpose.

Consider what happened when God was in deep relationship with someone on earth like Abraham or Moses. They were able to say something like, "Hang on! You can't do that! You can't wipe out all those people!" and they negotiated with Him. He wants us to realise that everything about this governmental aspect is relational and communal, and that the DIY tree path has corrupted those patterns by excluding God from them. Only in relationship with God can we hope to see them function properly.

"I kept looking
Until thrones were set up,
And the Ancient of Days took His seat;
His garment was white as snow,
And the hair of His head like pure wool.
His throne was ablaze with flames,
Its wheels were a burning fire.

A river of fire was flowing
And coming out from before Him;
Thousands upon thousands were serving Him,
And myriads upon myriads were standing before Him;
The court convened,
And the books were opened" (Daniel 7:9-10).

Here, God is depicted as a time-transcending judge sitting enthroned among other judges. Remember that judgment is always to life from God's perspective, never to death. It is we who have correlated His judgment with punishment; His judgments are always positive because they are based on the reality of the lamb slain before the foundation of the world.

We can find many different names for the members of these heavenly courts: they are called the holy ones, spirits, messengers, ministers, servants, princes and other names, often indicating their particular governmental or royal position. Some of these biblical titles for council members affirm the idea of semi-divinity, and this is where some people may become uneasy. They are referred to as *elohim* (gods, divine beings); and as *benei elohim*, *benei elim*, and *benei elyon* (sons of God, sons of the Most High). See Genesis 6:2; Psalms 8:5-6; 29:1; 82:6; 86:8; 89:7; 97:7; 138:1; Job 38:7.

None of this is any kind of threat to God's sovereignty. He is *Elohim*, and He is not threatened by His children being transformed into His image. Nor are we appropriating the glory of God: He gave it to us in the first place. He wants us to be like Him; He made us to be like Him; and He is longing for us to come into the fullness of the knowledge of Him and to live as His sons.

When charged with blasphemy for calling Himself the Son of God, Jesus pointed out to the Jewish religious leaders that their own scriptures described people as gods too:

Jesus answered them, "Has it not been written in your Law: 'I said, you are gods'? If he called them gods, to whom the word of God came (and the Scripture cannot be nullified), are you saying

197

of Him whom the Father sanctified and sent into the world, 'You are blaspheming,' because I said, 'I am the Son of God'?" (John 10:34-36).

God is very happy for us to be called 'gods' or 'sons of God' because we are made in His image and His likeness. This is why we really need to know who we are because we will shy away from it if we feel we have to make ourselves worthy. We do not. We are not saying, "Hey, look at us! We're gods!" We are saying, "Look at Jesus! Look at the Father! We are made in His image and we are going to fulfil our role as sons of God!"

The names of God

God, too, is referred to in many different ways which illustrate His role: Creator, Father, King, Judge, Lord and so on. In sonship, we receive the revelation that we are made in His image, according to His name. All His names have a meaning with which we can engage in order to be more fully conformed to His image.

These are the heavenly, transcendent names:

EL or *ELOAH*: God "mighty, strong, prominent" (Nehemiah 9:17; Psalm 139:19).

EL SHADDAI: "God Almighty," "The Mighty One of Jacob" (Genesis 49:24; Psalm 132:2, 5).

ELOHIM: God "Creator, mighty and strong" (Genesis 17:7; Jeremiah 31:33).

ADONAI: "Lord" (Genesis 15:2; Judges 6:15) – sometimes used in place of *YHWH*, thought to be too sacred to be uttered. *YHWH* is a covenant name, thus *Adonai* is more often used in His dealings with Gentiles.

YHWH or *YAHWEH*: "LORD" (Deuteronomy 6:4; Daniel 9:14). Revealed to Moses as 'I AM THAT I AM.' This name suggests an immediacy, a presence. "Jehovah" was an earlier (poor) transliteration. Some English Bibles show it as "LORD" (with small capitals in the body of the word) to distinguish it from *Adonai*, which they render as "Lord" (with normal case).

EL ELYON: "Most High" (Deuteronomy 26:19). Derives from the root 'go up, ascend,' which we are invited to do.

El ROI: "God who sees," a name ascribed to Him by Hagar (Genesis 16:13).

EL OLAM: "Enduring God" (Psalm 90:1-3).

EL GIBOR: "Mighty God" (Isaiah 9:6).

And these are all the compound names related to YHWH in covenant, which are the earthly, immanent names:

YAHWEH-JIREH: "The LORD Will Provide" (Genesis 22:14).

YAHWEH-RAPHA: "The LORD Who Heals" (Exodus 15:26).

YAHWEH-NISSI: "The LORD My Banner" (Exodus 17:15) (a banner is a rallying place).

YAHWEH-M'KADDESH: "The LORD Who Sanctifies, Makes Holy" (Leviticus 20:8; Ezekiel 37:28).

YAHWEH-SHALOM: "The LORD Is Peace" (Judges 6:24).

YAHWEH-ELOHIM: "LORD God" (Genesis 2:4; Psalm 59:5). The combination of these two names indicates that He is "Lord of Lords".

YAHWEH-TSIDKENU: "The LORD Our Righteousness" (Jeremiah 33:16).

YAHWEH-ROHI: "The LORD Our Shepherd" (Psalm 23:1).

YAHWEH-SHAMMAH: "The Lord Is There" (Ezekiel 48:35)

YAHWEH-SABAOTH: "The Lord of Hosts, the Lord of Armies" (Isaiah 1:24; Psalm 46:7).

When I first saw this list of names, many years ago, I thought I needed to study hard to understand each of them. Study has nothing to do with what I am proposing here. We have been

199

predestined to be conformed to His image in sonship: as we experience the reality of these names in relationship with Him, we can become transformed into that image.

We are to ascend as sons through our relationship with Father, Son and Spirit that reveals His essence, nature and character through His precepts, statutes and laws. Those are the three foundational elements of government, and when you take cases to a higher level court, you need to base all your court cases on the precepts, statutes and laws of God. Ultimately we are to ascend through all the twelve High Chancellors' Houses to become co-creators with our Father. Meanwhile, we may be assigned roles as a judge, magistrate, ambassador, chancellor or any number of other roles.

Heaven's court system

The secret [sod] of the Lord is for those who fear Him, And He will make them know His covenant (Psalm 25:14).

As I was in the prime of my days, When the friendship [sod] of God was over my tent; (Job 29:4).

The *sod* of the Lord is for those who honour and respect Him, and apparently Job fulfilled that requirement. And for us, the full revelation of the New Covenant is opened up in the *Sod* of God. As you see, the word '*sod*' may be translated into English in a number of different ways, including: circle, company, fellowship, friendship, secret, and secret counsel. That may help us grasp one level of meaning but hinder us from seeing the deeper truth, unless we know it is the *sod* that is being referenced. We can have access to the counsel of God as His trusted sons, learn His secret plan of restoration, and participate in the decision-making to see that plan fulfilled.

"Thus says the LORD of hosts, 'If you will walk in My ways and if you will perform My service, then you will also govern My house and also have charge of My courts, and I will grant you free access among these who are standing here'" (Zechariah 3:7).

We are all called to ascend to mature sonship, to access and have charge of the courts. In this scripture, as we have seen, the process is laid out for us: learn to walk with Him in the intimacy of fellowship and relationship; start doing the things He assigns us to do as lords; begin to rule and govern; have charge of the courts, and then we will start to operate freely in our designated roles in the councils and assemblies of God.

Look at this diagram of heaven's court system. We may not yet be functioning members of these courts (few of us are), but we can all have access to them. I have been into all of them: some many times, others more rarely. The diagram shows them arranged in levels, which correspond to different heavenly realms.

Heaven's Court System

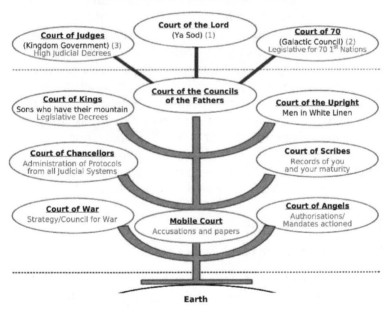

The Court of War, the Mobile Court and the Court of Angels operate on the level of the kingdom of God realm. That level we have to cleanse, because it is where the accusations are brought and the enemy has access to it. Dragons, giants and other representations of enemy activity are there, maybe even usurping our thrones, but they can go no higher because they have been excluded from the way to the Tree of Life.

On the next level, in the kingdom of heaven realm, are the Court of Chancellors and the Court of Scribes (where legislation gets agreed and written into the statute books). Then the realm of heaven itself, in which are the Court of Kings, the Court of Councils of the Fathers and the Court of the Upright (the men in white linen). Finally there are three courts in the realm of the heaven of heavens, which are the Court of Judges, the Court of the Lord (the *Ya Sod*) and the Court of Seventy (sometimes called the Galactic Council).

A word of caution: it is important that we do not exaggerate our role or our level of competence in our own minds. Some people have learned all these terms second-hand from others and think they can therefore sit in the Court of Judges or the Galactic Council. No, we have to mature into that. If someone does not want the trouble of going through the process of attaining maturity and just wants it all now, then I am sorry, it does not work that way. God is not about to allow anyone immature to go in and make judgments in those higher courts. We have to go through a process of learning to make righteous judgments in our own life, and then perhaps corporately with others with more experience. Eventually, when we have been faithful with the lesser responsibilities we have been given, we can progress to the greater ones.

Members of the Sod

So for now, who are in the Sod of God?

- Angelic heavenly representatives
- Ancient ones, sons of Adam who did not fall
- Enoch (pre-flood)
- Abraham (post-flood), representing all the families of the earth
- Moses
- Elijah

These are the ones I have seen. They are God's trusted representatives there, who have a vested interest in certain aspects of creation.

By faith Enoch was taken up so he would not see death; and he was not found because God took him up; for he obtained a witness that before his being taken up he was pleasing to God (Hebrews 11:5).

Enoch is there because he was pleasing to God. When God opens up heaven and says to you, "In you I am well pleased," it is because He wants you to live in the affirmation of His sonship and begin to mature into all He has planned for you as His son.

We can engage the *Sod* of God to re-engage the memory of our identity, of our scroll, of who we were before we came into this dimension and the destiny we agreed. If that is going too far for you, that is all right; you can leave it for now, ask the Father about it, and pursue it if and when you are ready.

The testimony record is also in the wine room in the Court of Scribes.

Helpers

"For I say to you that their angels in heaven continually see the face of my Father who is in heaven" (Matthew 18:10b).

We also have heavenly angels who have looked into the face of God on our behalf, and who occupy some of our positions in the courts of heaven, waiting for us to mature. So there is a connection, not just with our guardian angels but with other angels in these courts; and if we connect with them, they can be really helpful to us.

When I first started going onto my mountain and sitting on my throne, I was not really bothered about what it looked like – I am not really interested in aesthetics of things, I just want to get on and do the business. So I would sit on my throne, wearing my crown, and do whatever I needed to. But then

COURT OF THE LORD

when I began doing activations with other people, taking them in with me, I had time to look around. I looked at my throne, and there behind it was a huge angel. I asked him, "Who are you?" I had never even noticed he was there before.

He said, "I am the angel who has been in this position assigned to you in heaven, who has caretaken this position for you in the kingdom. I am here to advise you how to rule." Sometimes you get those moments when you think "Ah! Why didn't I think of that before?" But at least now I was able to engage him, and soon I discovered other angels in positions that are intended for me, who have also been there just waiting for me to mature. And you also have angels waiting there for you. They have insight and revelation to help you, which is encouraging if, as I was, you are starting off with absolutely no idea how to do anything.

Are they not all ministering spirits, sent out to render service for the sake of those who will inherit salvation? (Hebrews 1:14).

There are other beings who are available to us too. I found Wisdom to be the most amazing person to teach you to come into your position of government. She showed me how to do everything in the courts. She took me to the Court of Kings, and there was a scroll, the first law I produced. She showed me that we needed to go to the Chancellor's Court to get it agreed, and then to the Court of Scribes to get it written into the record. I was clueless about how to do any of that. She showed me and she will show you, if that is something you need to do. No doubt she will also show you other things that I have not done and other places I have not been.

But I know that you can engage the Court of the Upright and other courts, and that when I have engaged the Court of the Council of the Fathers, it has been to receive mandates. At the beginning of 2016, the Father said, "I want you to legislate. I want you to give me time to legislate every day, to make laws." I had to find out how to do that, so I sought out Wisdom and she told me to go to the Court of the Council of the Fathers. I saw two sets of twelve elders there, and I said to them, "I have this assignment from God. Where do I start?" They gave me a whole lot of legislative advice to go away and engage with.

Another time, I was told to do a court case in the Court of Seventy. Again I spent a lot of time with Wisdom and again she took me to the Court of the Council of the Fathers. I told them, "I need to know what I am authorised to do, and at what level. I don't want to step outside of my jurisdiction." It took me 18 months to learn how to do it. Maybe I was just slow on the uptake, but there was a lot to learn. I spent time going back there, seeking Wisdom, receiving the revelation and then allowing that revelation to birth something. Eventually I was able to make that case in the Court of Seventy.

Activation #13: Let Jesus take you

Again, you can use the text or the audio. Follow the same basic pattern of engagement we have used before and ask Jesus to take you where you need to go in this process. Step into heaven, and let's see.

Consciously relax and surrender.

We have an open heaven.
We know Jesus has torn the veil
so we have an invitation to come.

Close your eyes.
Think about those steps.
Choose to engage
and by faith take a step into the realm of heaven.
Go through the veil.

If you do not see this as a vision, do not be concerned; just trust that your spirit will be engaging and that you will be receiving spiritually even if perhaps at the moment your mind is not ready to accept everything. Just by faith, engage.

205

Whether you are seeing it, feeling it, sensing it or knowing it
does not really matter. Be willing to engage by faith.

As you step through the door
Jesus is there waiting.

Now we present ourselves to Him
surrendering any agenda we might have
(we want His agenda).

Ask Jesus to take you where He wants to take you.
(If your heart is set on engaging the Court of the Lord,
ask Him if He will take you there).

Let Him take you by the hand
Let Him lead you
Let Him guide you.

He will take you through the veils
if you are going to engage in the various courts,
or maybe you are going to engage
the judgment seat of Christ with your scroll.
Just be open to whatever experience you need right now.

So if it's engaging the Court of the Lord,
coming before the very presence of God there
then be willing to engage that.
Maybe engaging your scroll,
coming under the Shepherd's rod.

Maybe asking Jesus to introduce you
to some of those angels that are representing you
in the different courts of heaven.
So many different things you could experience.

Just be led by Jesus
to engage in any one of these places
to really reconnect with your sonship
to bring you into a position of maturity
and help you on your journey,
and in your process.

15. The Order of Melchizedek

I began by outlining the four dimensions in which we can engage with the Father:

1. In the earth, the physical realm, under an open heaven.
2. In our spirit and heart, the spiritual dimension.
3. In the heavenly realms.
4. In eternity, outside of time and space.

In the course of this book we have at least touched on all four, and as we continue to engage with Him we will become more confident to go further and deeper. We have also considered our purpose in engaging the Father: primarily to develop and enjoy the relationship, fellowship and intimacy of sonship. However, God's original intention was for earth to be like heaven, so our sonship also brings the responsibility that flows from intimacy, first entrusted to Adam and Eve:

God blessed them; and God said to them, "Be fruitful and multiply, and fill the earth, and subdue it; and rule over the fish of the sea and over the birds of the sky and over every living thing that moves on the earth" (Genesis 1:28).

God blessed them (He empowered them to prosper and to be successful), and in blessing them He commissioned them to be fruitful, to multiply and fill the earth, to overcome any hindrances and to rule. He was not telling Adam and Eve to rule over other people: He was empowering mankind to fulfil our responsibility of ensuring that our world is just like heaven, aligned with God's original intention and purpose.

God's government

We find our identity in relationship; identity brings position; and position brings authority from heaven. As sons, made in the image of God, we have this sonship mandate and have been given responsibility for a kingdom that is being raised up to fill the earth and so increase God's government and peace.

We fulfil our responsibility as sons by using the authority of our position to administrate it. In conventional church settings people do not really talk about government at all; if they do, it usually refers to the church leadership. But kingdom is all about government: it is all about bringing God's will from heaven to earth.

Nebuchadnezzar dreamed of a stone crushing a statue which had a head of gold, chest of silver, thighs of bronze and feet of iron and clay. That statue represented four empires, of which the last was the Roman (iron representing the western part, and clay the eastern). The stone was Jesus; a stone cut without hands from the mountain (representing authority); the stone struck the statue's feet, the whole thing collapsed, and the stone became a great mountain that filled the whole earth.

The message of the kingdom, the message of love, was taken out to the whole (known) world within a generation. And today, even by conservative estimates, there are well over a billion people who call themselves Christians. If you think of a group of eleven disciples and then a few hundred people who watched as Jesus went back into heaven, a billion is quite an increase. We cannot be satisfied with that number, though, because we have not really transformed the earth. We have been side-tracked into creating a religion (and the thousands of its variations) rather than actually fulfilling the mandate God gave us.

"How great are His signs
And how mighty are His wonders!
His kingdom is an everlasting kingdom
And His dominion is from generation to generation"
(Daniel 4:3).

God is restoring that mandate and restoring us to the position of authority, and it will fill the earth. That can happen in our generation, in the next generation, or it may take a hundred generations, but it will fill the earth. How soon depends at least in part upon whether we will respond in sonship and start fulfilling our roles in the kingdom. God's purpose is to bring His kingdom into the earth through generations who will embrace it.

Historically, when a generation has embraced something it has then tended to enshrine it in stone and defend it against whatever revelation the next generation brings, rather than recognising what God is doing, supporting it, embracing it, and doing it together. God wants to change all that with us, which is why we want to be sure not to go back into the old way of thinking.

"And to Him was given dominion,
Glory and a kingdom,
That all the peoples, nations and men of every language
Might serve Him.
His dominion is an everlasting dominion
Which will not pass away;
And His kingdom is one
Which will not be destroyed (Daniel 7:14).

Ultimately 'church' may collapse into a religious institution but His kingdom will not. We are part of that kingdom, sons of that kingdom; we are responsible for the outworking of the government of the kingdom of God because we are those mandated with the authority:

But the saints of the Highest One will receive the kingdom
and possess the kingdom forever [alema], for all ages to com.
(Daniel 7:18).

That word *alema* (from *olam*) does not really mean 'forever' but 'enduring to the ages'. So this kingdom will go on for all the ages, but that does not mean eternally or forever. We are here to fulfil God's kingdom in this age and to usher in the next age.

A great deal is being taught about 'the church age' and 'the kingdom age' but let's be careful that does not descend into elitism. God does work in seasons, but He does not stop working with people in the old season when a new season

209

comes: He continues working with them until they embrace the new one. There are probably hundreds of millions of Christians who have never experienced intimacy with the Father or with Jesus. Is God going to give up on those people? No, He is going to keep calling them, keep wooing them into deeper relationship with Him.

We are going to see the kingdom at work until it has finished fulfilling God's purpose; then Jesus will hand it over to the Father; and we will move on into further increase of His government, because there will be no end to the increase of His government or of peace (see Isaiah 9:7).

The mountain of the house of the Lord

Now it will come about that in the last days the mountain of the house of the Lord will be established as the chief of the mountains, and will be raised above the hills; and all the nations will stream to it (Isaiah 2:2).

A mountain is a symbol of kingdom governmental authority, and that authority now resides with us. The 'last days' were the last days of the Old Covenant, a generation during which the New Covenant was already established and was beginning to fill the earth. So now we are fully in the New, although religion keeps going back to the old and attempting to reinstitute the same old mediatorial priesthood on earth, which is not God's desire.

There has been a lot of talk about mountains over the last several years, especially around the 'seven mountains' theology. I do not believe that man-made mountains can be redeemed, so trying to take over the world's media mountain, government mountain, business mountain and so on is not going to solve the world's problems. If you are personally called to outwork the kingdom through your life and work in one of those spheres, and are able to exercise godly authority in that position, that is a completely different matter. But those worldly systems are not the kingdom.

210

Eventually people will start to realise that they are not going to find their solutions in man-made things. Whatever those authorities are, they are not God and they are not the kingdom. I do not want to prop up a worldly system, I want to demonstrate a better kingdom, the relational kingdom of God. Now the mountains of the world are hills, because the mountain of the house of the Lord is operating in the higher realms of heaven. Individually of course we are each a house of the Lord but we are also being corporately built together with living stones into a holy temple. Not just one local church, or one denomination or stream, but all of us.

People are looking for something more; most of them do not know what that might be. I spent virtually the whole of my life searching, until I engaged heaven and found where I was birthed to be and called to be as a son. That is why there is going to be a streaming to us when we are raised up as the mountain of the house of the Lord.

We are the Joshua, Joseph, Daniel and Enoch generation. And you can throw a few other names in there, not least that of David. In David's Tabernacle the presence of God was openly displayed in the midst of the people and they could all worship freely. It was looking forward to the New Covenant, but what have we done? We have gone back to shutting God up in church buildings, or cathedrals, or meeting rooms or whatever else. God is restoring David's Tabernacle in our day: He wants to be openly displayed again before the whole world, through us, His people; so that wherever we are, there is a representation of God's kingdom.

We are the *ekklesia*, living stones who represent God 24/7 wherever we are and not just when we turn up at a church meeting (even if that is 4 or 5 times a week). I absolutely believe in having an expression of the kingdom of God to bless our communities through a local church (though again let me emphasise that *ekklesia* really is a much better name for it because when people – believers or not – hear the word 'church' they already have an image of what it means. And whether it has positive or negative connotations for them, it

211

certainly does not adequately represent what I am describing here).

We are being called to be seated in heavenly places as sons, legislating, governing and administrating to see that 'as it is in heaven' on earth. So we are going to need to exercise our mandate for dominion as sons. There is a sharp intake of breath from some quarters as soon as you start talking about dominion, government or rule. The word 'dominion' in particular seems to trigger people because of so-called 'dominion theology'. This is nothing to do with dominion theology.

Dominion is a biblical term, if that matters to you, and we have already seen it several times. The word appears in Daniel 4:3, where 'the Most High God' has dominion; and Daniel 7:18, in which 'One like a Son of Man' is given dominion, and the King James translation of Genesis 1:28, in which Adam and Eve are given dominion.

Where I am

This hope we have as an anchor of the soul, a hope both sure and steadfast and one which enters within the veil, where Jesus has entered as a forerunner for us, having become a high priest forever according to the order of Melchizedek (Hebrews 6:19-20).

In My Father's house are many mansions; if it were not so, I would have told you. I go to prepare a place for you. And if I go and prepare a place for you, I will come again and receive you to Myself; that where I am, there you may be also (John 14:2-3 NKJV).

If you were to quote those passages in a religious setting, most likely they would be interpreted as saying that when we die we can go to heaven because Jesus has gone there to prepare the way. Specifically, that He is preparing mansions for us in heaven, so that when we go there we will have a home.

That is not how I read them at all. In John 14, we are the mansions, we are the house(s) of God. Jesus is not in heaven preparing some mansion: Jesus is in the Father, preparing us to be a dwelling place for Him. That is why He went to the cross, so that 'Where I am (i.e. in the Father), you may be also.' So much scripture has been translated within a framework of understanding which puts it off to the future. What was indeed future for the first century audience is often for us either a present reality or even the distant past.

"I am going to prepare a place for you" is a phrase from the Hebrew marriage contract. A *ketubah* was made, outlining the couple's expectations of the marriage. After it was agreed, they would sign it, stand to face each other and say:

> Bridegroom: "I go to prepare a place for you; that where I am, there you may be also."
>
> Bride: "When will you come back to receive me to yourself?"
>
> Bridegroom: "I do not know the day or the hour, but when my father approves the wedding chamber, he will send me back to receive you unto myself."

Then the bridegroom would go away and build a house (usually attached to his father's house, as was the custom). When the bridegroom's father agreed that the house was ready the marriage would proceed. Jesus went to the cross to prepare us to be a place of His dwelling, so that we would be where He is, in I AM. 'Where He is' is not heaven. 'Where He is' is about relationship, and none of this has anything to do with 'going to heaven when you die.'

Order of Melchizedek

But Jesus has entered within the veil as a forerunner for us, so that we can enter too. He has done this by 'having become a high priest forever according to the order of Melchizedek.' So what is the order of Melchizedek? It is a function of the office of priest and king: a heavenly function, a priestly function and a kingly function.

213

For this Melchizedek, king of Salem, priest of the Most High God, who met Abraham as he was returning from the slaughter of the kings and blessed him, to whom also Abraham apportioned a tenth part of all the spoils, was first of all, by the translation of his name, king of righteousness, and then also king of Salem, which is king of peace. Without father, without mother, without genealogy, having neither beginning of days nor end of life, but made like the Son of God, he remains a priest perpetually (Hebrews 7:1-3).

I do not believe Melchizedek is the pre-incarnate Christ, nor that he is Shem, another popular candidate. He is not a man at all – he has no genealogy: he is a spiritual being, a king and a priest who operates in the heavenly realms. I believe he was one of the covering cherubs and is chief Chancellor of the house of God's Treasury. He has a very key role in our sonship and in our manifesting heaven on earth. But the real issue is not so much about the person of Melchizedek himself: instead let us focus on Jesus. Jesus is a heavenly high priest, of the order of Melchizedek: He could not be a priest of the Aaronic order because He was not of the right tribe. In any case, that earthly order is obsolete, and we now have this new heavenly order, the order of Melchizedek. If we are also to be part of that heavenly order, we have to have our genealogy dealt with so that we are not earthly.

We need transformation at all levels, which is why communion is so powerful: the body and blood of Jesus transforms us. It begins to change this earthly body into the transfigured body that Jesus demonstrated on the mountain, radiating with light, so that we can live forever[13] – and I for one certainly plan to do so. And as we ascend and engage with the nine strands of God's DNA, we will become fully formed sons and begin to take on the image of our Father.

---

[13] See our blog post *188. Live And Not Die* at freedomarc.blog

Heaven to earth

But you are a chosen people, a royal priesthood, a holy nation, a people for God's own possession, so that you may proclaim the excellencies of Him who has called you out of darkness into His marvelous light (1 Peter 2:9).

"You have made them to be a kingdom and priests to our God; and they will reign upon the earth" (Revelation 5:10).

The kingly, priestly function is a manifestation of the same sonship mandate given to Adam and Eve, to be responsible for the earth. So we are of that heavenly order but then we are to bring heaven to earth in agreement. We operate as kings and priests in heaven; and as oracles and legislators on the earth. We are the full representation of the four faces of God, fully representing Him in heaven and fully representing Him here on earth - so that is the fullness of His government.

"Your kingdom come.
Your will be done,
On earth as it is in heaven" (Matthew 6:10).

We get to be involved in the 'as it is in heaven' as kings and priests. If we are trying to rule on the earth without establishing in heaven first, that will never work. This is why the Joshua generation operates according to the order of Melchizedek beyond the torn veil, as forerunners of this heavenly royal priesthood: to prepare the next generation to embrace their inheritance as sons of God too; to come into their authority, seated in heavenly positions of government, to rule and legislate from a place of intimacy and relationship with the Father into the earth.

It is all about bringing heaven to earth. It is a wonderful thing to engage with heaven and operate in heaven but ultimately what is the purpose of that if it does not change the earth? It just becomes some ethereal, esoteric experience that makes no earthly difference. Certainly we are in the very beginning of all this and we are not yet fully matured or fully functioning in the order of Melchizedek, so I am in this for the long haul

215

and not a quick fix. I believe it is going to take three generations working together but that does not necessarily mean that it will take another forty to eighty years. Even if it did, I plan to be around that long (in fact, I plan to live for ever) and I would like a lot of people to be around with me, because we have to administrate this to see God's kingdom established in a more consistent way.

For you have not come to a mountain that can be touched and to a blazing fire, and to darkness and gloom and whirlwind... But you have come to Mount Zion and to the city of the living God, the heavenly Jerusalem, and to myriads of angels, to the general assembly and church of the firstborn who are enrolled in heaven, and to God, the Judge of all, and to the spirits of the righteous made perfect, and to Jesus, the mediator of a new covenant, and to the sprinkled blood, which speaks better than the blood of Abel (Hebrews 12:18, 22-24).

In the Old Covenant, Israel could not touch the mountain because they had rejected relationship with God and chosen to do their own thing by sending Moses as a mediator. But we have come to Mount Zion, the mountain of God in heaven, the same mountain where the fire stones are and the garden of God is, a place of authority. The city of the living God is the New Jerusalem: there is both a heavenly and an earthly expression of that, It is not coming down out of heaven sometime in the future; it is already here now. We are the expression of the New Jerusalem.

And if anyone still objects that we should not engage with angels, the writer to the Hebrews says here that we can. The myriads are the angelic canopy and there are myriads upon myriads upon myriads of them. It goes on to speak of the general assembly and church of the firstborn enrolled in heaven and the spirits of the righteous made perfect, confirmation that we can indeed engage with those saints who are in heaven, the cloud of witnesses. And it culminates with God and with Jesus: how wonderful it is that He is a mediator of a new covenant and we do not have to be in the

216

old one! Beware of being drawn back in by the mixture of covenants which is so widespread in the church today.

Since the order of Melchizedek is priestly, it is involved in mediation; not mediation between people and God but mediation between heaven and earth. We are those in heaven mediating for creation, and for the earth to be restored to its original heavenly position by bringing heaven to earth in the form of the kingdom of God.

The order of Melchizedek is kingly, so it is governmental and legislative to the affairs of the nations of the world. We are called to disciple the nations: it has been ambiguously translated 'make disciples of all nations' but actually it says 'disciple the nations,' which is again bringing all the nations back into the mountain of the house of the Lord.

The order of Melchizedek has access to the mysteries of God, the resources of heaven's treasury; all that is in the different houses and library rooms of heaven, including the scroll room, the record room and the discovery room; and the revelation of the sapphire cube on the sapphire pavement. So much for us to discover, and we will be able to engage whichever of them we need to fulfil our mandate.

I went into the library room in 2010 and there was one light shining on one book. At that time I was hungry for knowledge, and God told me later that if He had shown me all the books back then I would never have left the library! When you read a book there you instantly absorb the content, just like Trinity acquiring the ability to fly a helicopter in the movie *The Matrix*. Some people are doing that sort of thing already: they do not know how to do something and when they read the book in the realm of heaven, they get to know how to do it without ever being taught, because the revelation and the knowledge is imparted in a heavenly way.

The order of Melchizedek reflects the four faces of God; it has access to the Holy of Holies and the revelation of the covering cherubim, releasing the revelation of the character and nature of God. It is a new covenant order: the kingly and priestly functions release heavenly apostolic blueprints which carry the purpose of God to be manifested in the earth. These blueprints are visionary descriptions of what God desires on the earth, and it is when we receive such blueprints that the government forms and we begin to outwork the vision.

The prophetic (oracle) and apostolic (legislation) operate together to form a foundation of the word of God and the government of God as a reflection on earth. Look again at this diagram which we saw in chapter 12.

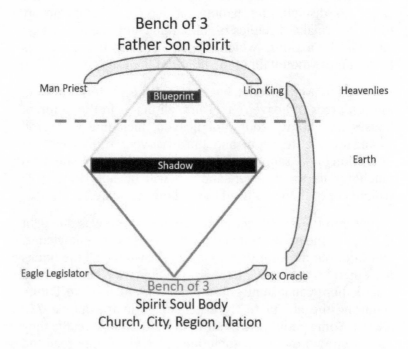

In heaven there is an arc of agreement between king and priest; we have a blueprint given to us and its shadow forms on the earth. We connect earth and heaven and form a foundation on the earth, bringing heaven and earth into agreement.

That is the government of the order of Melchizedek. There is no hierarchy: it is foundational government which releases everyone to fulfil their destiny and mandate. It keeps just expanding and expanding to fill the earth, the cosmos, and ultimately all of creation with the kingdom and glory of God.

16. Sons Arise!

Authority and glory

Each one of us, as a son seated in heavenly places on our mountain, on our throne, has a blueprint (a scroll, a destiny) that carries with it seven main spheres of governmental authority, and once we truly know our identity as sons then the next stage is to find out what we are authorised to do. Our mountains are often concerned with matters we already know and care about but have perhaps never thought of as spheres of authority. Some people have a mandate for worship; some for business; some for family; some people have a mandate for a particular area of ministry. I discovered that most of my mountains were ministry-orientated because that is a reflection of what God has called me to do. All of us have particular spheres of authority and it is good to find out what they are.

We are priests and kings in heaven with the governmental authority in, through and around our lives, and we are called to have dominion as a gateway of that authority into the earth. We may need to deal with some things in our earthly past; that will enable us to reconnect to our eternal past, revealing and drawing us into our future destiny.

The order of Melchizedek functions according to the governmental image of God, seated or enthroned in the heavenly places. Note that it is primarily a seated position: we are not frantically running around trying to make things happen. We are at rest and at peace in that position, which gives us the authority to administrate. The government of God is associated with the four living creatures and the four faces of God, which is why we did the activation engaging those four faces. As the order of Melchizedek we can stand in the name of God and operate in the fourfold function of the lion, ox, eagle and man.

Now above the expanse that was over their heads there was something resembling a throne, like lapis lazuli in appearance;

and on that which resembled a throne, high up, was a figure with the appearance of a man (Ezekiel 1:26).

We are that man. Now you could read it as Jesus or the Father sitting there; but this is a man, and it relates both to our thrones and to our own appearance in heaven.

As the appearance of the rainbow in the clouds on a rainy day, so was the appearance of the surrounding radiance. Such was the appearance of the likeness of the glory of the Lord (Ezekiel 1:28a).

We are made in the likeness of God, and it is our glory as sons that will bring the freedom for which creation is longing. So often we get caught up with acknowledging that the glory belongs to the Lord (because indeed it does: His glory belongs to Him), but in the same way, our glory belongs to us. Glory is the weight or essence of something. His glory is fatherhood; our glory is sonship.

For the anxious longing of the creation waits eagerly for the revealing of the sons of God. For the creation was subjected to futility, not willingly, but because of Him who subjected it, in hope that the creation itself also will be set free from its slavery to corruption into the freedom of the glory of the children of God (Romans 8:19-21).

We must find and outwork our identity because we will never radiate our glory for creation to respond to if we do not know who we are (and if we are thinking that it is all about God alone rather than God in relationship with us). God has assigned us to do these things, but for generations we have been calling out on Him to rend the heavens and come down. I remember praying it over and over again: "Rend the heavens and come down! Please, please, come and bless us!" He has already rent the heavens. He has come down, and He has gone up again. And now He is calling us to "Come up here." He is saying, "Why are you praying like that? I have already blessed you and empowered you to be seated here with Me."

221

He is waiting, and creation is waiting, for us to rise up and take our places. Sons, arise and know your identity! Sons, arise and know your authority! Be seated in your position! We can have confidence to enter the holy place by the blood of Jesus, so let's draw near. Let's engage with the Arc. Let's come and begin to see the manifestation of His presence. The earthly high priest did not just go in and then, all of a sudden, God was there. He had to engage the name of God. He sang the name of God: that created a frequency, a resonance, an electromagnetic energy which created a portal through which the manifestation of God would come. If no one is around the arc, God does not manifest. His presence is there because we are there: our engagement causes His presence to manifest.

The two covering cherubim looked into the deep things of God and they released the "holy, holy, holy" of His character and nature, so when we come close we are drawing close to the nature and character of God. The four beings, each with four faces, present sixteen dimensions of revelation of the nature of God: numbers are important in heaven. The four beings had six wings with four hands which is another 24 dimensions of revelation; and there are 96 dimensions of revelation in total for us to explore and discover. I do not think we are going to get to know it all by reading and studying the Bible, but only by engaging God more and more deeply.

... and in the middle of the lampstands I saw one like a son of man, clothed in a robe reaching to the feet, and girded across His chest with a golden sash. His head and His hair were white like white wool, like snow; and His eyes were like a flame of fire. His feet were like burnished bronze, when it has been made to glow in a furnace, and His voice was like the sound of many waters. In His right hand He held seven stars, and out of His mouth came a sharp two-edged sword; and His face was like the sun shining in its strength (Revelation 1:13-16).

Jesus is the Son of Man. This figure was 'like' a son of man: it is a description of how we are to be seen in heaven and how heaven sees us. The white hair symbolises wisdom; and we can speak with the voice of God which is like the sound of many waters; and heaven, earth, and all of creation listens and responds. The seven stars are positions of government in seven spheres of authority. The sharp two-edged sword is the word of God in our mouth, living and active. The shining face speaks of our transfiguration: we are spirit and light beings.

The heavenly tabernacle

Behind the second veil there was a tabernacle which is called the Holy of Holies, having a golden altar of incense and the ark of the covenant covered on all sides with gold, in which was a golden jar holding the manna, and Aaron's rod which budded, and the tables of the covenant; and above it were the cherubim of glory overshadowing the mercy seat (Hebrews 9:3-5a).

The pattern of the earthly tabernacle reveals the pattern of the heavenly, with the outer court, inner court and Holy of Holies. The heavenly tabernacle is strongly linked with the Order of Melchizedek; and it is the function of the Joshua Generation to be operating there. We are priests, and we have access to the Holy of Holies as the earthly high priest did.

We can all come and look into the arc to see what the Father is doing and to receive a mandate or authorisation. In the earthly arc were a jar of manna, Aaron's rod and the stone tablets. As I said, I spent a year looking at those three items and what they represent – the manna: the will of God; the tablets: covenant, God's law written on our hearts; and the rod: the sceptre of heavenly government – before I realised that there was so much more to engage with there, and began stepping into the four faces of God.

Every day now we can say, "I want to go to the place where I can engage the presence of God" and go there, because He is saying, "Come up here and engage with Me! In fact, live here and minister from here!" We go and engage inwards; and we minister outwards. We come in our royal robes, robes of righteousness; not to beg for mercy, but in the confidence of sonship. We engage, behold and become transformed, so that earth too can be transformed to resemble heaven, and heaven and earth will overlap as they were always intended to do in the plans and purposes of God.

We engage the tabernacle in the heavens and we are now the tabernacle on earth: we are the house of God and we are also being built together into a holy temple of God on earth. Not a religious temple, but a group of people who are living stones, living together in relationship, being built up in love to demonstrate God's kingdom.

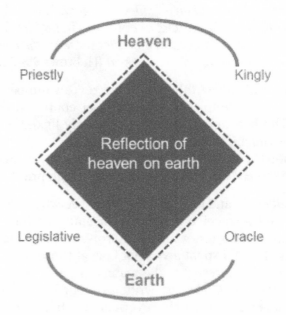

When we have this agreement, this arc between heaven and earth, we will then see heaven reflected on earth. Its shape is the base of a pyramid, the shape of the New Jerusalem, the shape of the mountain of God. And when heaven and earth are in agreement, the mountain of the house of the Lord is raised up.

There is a blueprint or a scroll for our individual lives and also for gathering together around that blueprint as an *ekklesia*. In fact, there will be a blueprint for whatever else God calls us to do.

There are many patterns that God shows us to help us outwork our destiny and bring heaven to earth:

2 = an arc of agreement. When two come into agreement that opens a portal for an experiential manifestation.

3 = government and manifestation of the kingdom at hand.

4 = an open window or doorway, enabling the kingdom to manifest. This is essential for seeing heaven on earth.

1 + 1 + 1 = 3. Father, Son and Spirit. A bench of 3 is government.

3 + 1 = 4. God's government plus mankind's agreement makes the window. We come into agreement with God to being heaven to earth.

3 x 3 = 9. The number of completion.

9 stones covering the light bearer's body as he stood as the covering cherub. 9 stones of revelation to ascend.

9 + 3 = 12. Heaven and earth in harmony and fullness of government. God is complete in Himself, but He has chosen for the fullness of His government to be 12:

- 12 tribes of Israel
- 12 stones on the High Priest's breastplate
- revelation of 3 additional stones of ascension to make a total of 12 fire stones
- 12 foundational stones in the New Jerusalem.

Biblical numerology, the power of agreement, frequencies of light, colour, sound, vibrational movement, open portals, veils – this is so much fun compared to my life in the Brethren Church! I used to go every Sunday morning, sit down and be miserable for my sins that were 'killing Jesus'. There was no life in it. This is an adventure, a quest; and one that is to be pursued with passion and zeal so that we can bring heaven and earth back together into superimposition and overlap.

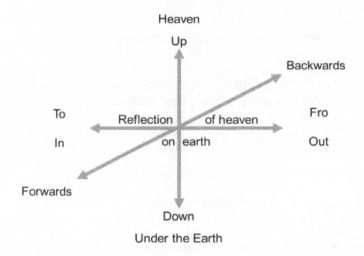

When we are engaging in heaven, and in the four faces of God, we have access to go up into that realm of heaven; access to come down, and bring things down from heaven into the earth. In that going up and coming down we bring about the reflection of heaven on earth. We have access to go in and out, and to go to and fro; backwards and forwards in space and time. No limits: all the boundaries are removed and we can access eternity, walking back on that ancient path.

The priestly function is to engage the heart of God in intimacy and get to know His heart; then we can discuss with Him how to bring about the outworking of His will and purpose. We can talk to Him. He actually wants us to interact with Him as sons with our Father. Everything is not fixed and settled without our input: we have a significant part to play. We can access the *Ya Sod* and the other courts of heaven to be involved in the planning.

And then once we have that agreement in the heart we can operate in the kingly function, bringing that agreement out of heaven into the earth to prepare for the earthly manifestation.

So we need to see the manifest presence of the glory of God. I love the presence of God but I want His glory; that is why I want to be in heaven when I engage God. Sometimes we pray, "O God, show us your glory." Glory clouds may appear in our meetings, which is wonderful, but where is the manifestation of heaven on earth? Because that is the real glory of God. It is not just a cloud. When the cloud came and filled Solomon's temple, the priests could not even stand, but Jude says we will stand and minister in the glory.

We look into the manifest presence and glory of God.
We see the will and purpose of God for our lives.
We resonate with His will and align ourselves to it.
Our hearts' desires draw us towards His will and our destiny.

We receive our mandate to rule.
We begin to frame our world from the mandate we receive.
We become the representation of the four faces, the four functions of priest, king; oracle and legislator on earth.
We act as kings and priests.
We speak prophetically as an oracle and administer legislation.

We can stand in the four faces of God's government, as sons, in the power of attorney of His name.
We can see through the lion's eyes; we can speak with the lion's voice.
So too with the eyes and voice of the Ox, Eagle and Man.

We are in the place of what is God's heavenly perspective: What Is.
We have access to God's eternal perspective: What Was Was before there was.

We have access to the Beginning and the End,
Alpha and Omega,
The Aleph and the Tav.

We do not just have to say "O God, will you lead me today!" and hope everything will work out. We are sons. We are co-heirs with Christ. We can begin to frame our world and frame our lives from the mandate we are given. I do not just hope for the best, I expect the favour of God around my life so I decree it and call it into being. If there is something I need, I call it to manifest: I call it as if it is, even when it is not yet –

because that is what God did when He created everything: He called 'things that be not as though they were' (see Romans 4:17 KJV). We have the same authority, so we can create the atmosphere of blessing and kingdom around our lives to manifest heaven on earth.

And if there is opposition, then we rule over it and subdue it. If there is a legal reason for that opposition, we can go to the mobile court, find out what that reason is, and get a verdict which gives us authority to change it and not be subject to it. Some people are praying the same way they used to pray, interceding as they used to intercede, and are not getting the results they used to get. The old ways do not work for us anymore once the new has come (even if they still work for others, at least for a while).

We are not victims: we are rulers. If we are not ruling and not governing then we are allowing whatever is happening around our lives. The accuser will take advantage of us if we allow it. God used to just protect us from a lot of this, but now He is encouraging us to start ruling, governing, administrating, restoring, and bringing alignment with heaven on earth around our lives.

So let's stop tagging 'in the name of Jesus' onto the end of our prayers like a lucky charm, hoping that will make them more effective. Most of those prayers are not in the name of Jesus anyway, they are in our name, because we are asking for help or asking God to do something. Instead, we now stand in the name of Jesus in the four faces, in *Yod Hei Vav Hei*, in the place of authority; and we use the power we have as sons of God to decree and declare and call things into being, to manifest those things on earth as we are declaring them in heaven.

We are the priests and the kings now. We can engage and discover God's eternal love relationship and dance. We can engage and discover the heart of God for our lives and for all creation. We can engage and discover God's desire for the restoration and continual realignment of all things.

God has set eternity into our hearts (see Ecclesiastes 3:11) to draw us back into this place of heavenly authority because it is where we will find we belong, where we were created to be. This is where I had been looking for all my life. I want to see God's kingdom on earth as it is in heaven. I want to see it in my life, my city and my nation. And wherever you are in the world as you read this, I want to see it in your life, your city and your nation too, as I am sure you do. So embrace this!

Activation #14: Arc of the Presence

Let's do a final activation together: come and step into the Arc of the presence of God, step into His name; see from His perspective, through the eyes of the lion, ox, eagle and man. Listen to the audio on the resources page or follow the text.

Begin to fix your eyes on that open heaven.
Step into it,
and by faith ask Jesus to take you to that place
of engaging the Arc of His presence.

If you don't know how to get there, He will take you.
You are taking a step of faith and you are stepping into it
- go for it!

As you stand there,
engage with the lion, ox, eagle and man.
Sense their presence by faith.
Engage with them now.

You may receive mandates today
for cities, for areas,
for your life, for your family, for *ekklesias*.

You might be given blueprints today for new things.
Be open to receive something;
let your spirit take it in.

Take those scrolls and receive them.
And then be willing to stand in the name of God
in *Yod Hei Vav Hei*,
in the lion, ox, eagle, man.

Start to look out.
See through the eyes of the lion
or the eagle or the ox or the man.

Let your spirit rise up.
Sons of God, arise! take your place!

And from that place, release heaven through you.
Start to decree things over your life.
Start to declare the government of God.
Start, as a priest, to catch the heart of God and release it.
Release those scrolls.

You may want to walk back into eternity.

Wherever this gives access for you,
just be open for this engagement.
Allow God, through this, to engage you
and just go into this experience.

I want to encourage you to just go for this! Whether or not
you experience it cognitively, whether or not you understand
everything, just let your spirit engage: that is the key.

Stay there for as long as you wish, and return over and over
again.

Further resources

Books

Mike Parsons' previous books, *My Journey Beyond Beyond* (2018), *The Restoration of All Things* (2021) and *The Eschatology of the Restoration of All Things* (2022) are all available from local and online booksellers.

For more details visit our website:

eg.freedomarc.org/books

Look out for more titles in this *Sons Arise!* series coming soon.

Other media

Engaging God: our self-paced monthly subscription programme for the Joshua Generation. For your two-week free trial visit eg.freedomarc.org/subscribe-to-engaging-god

Patreon: your opportunity to partner with us in taking the message of God's unconditional love, limitless grace and triumphant mercy to all His children. Become a patron at patreon.com/freedomarc to join Mike and other patrons for monthly group Zooms and other benefits.

Mike's YouTube channel: new videos are normally posted daily. View and subscribe at freedomarc.org/youtube

Sons of Issachar blog: shorter written articles drawn from Mike's teaching and online conversations. Read and subscribe at freedomarc.blog

Social media: follow Freedom ARC at

freedomarc.org/facebook

freedomarc.org/twitter

freedomarc.org/instagram

freedomarc.org/pinterest

Acknowledgements

Unless otherwise noted, scripture quotations are taken from the (NASB®) New American Standard Bible®, Copyright © 1960, 1971, 1977, 1995, 2020 by The Lockman Foundation. Used by permission. All rights reserved. www.lockman.org

Other versions referenced:

AMP: Scripture taken from the Amplified Bible, Copyright © 2015 by The Lockman Foundation. Used by permission.

AMPC: Scripture taken from the Amplified Bible, Classic Edition. Copyright © 1954, 1958, 1962, 1964, 1965, 1987 by The Lockman Foundation. Used by permission. www.lockman.org.

Mirror: The Mirror Bible. Copyright © 2017, 2021 by Francois Du Toit. Used by kind permission of the author. All rights reserved.

NKJV: Scripture taken from the New King James Version®. Copyright © 1982 by Thomas Nelson. Used by permission. All rights reserved.

OJB: Scripture taken from the Orthodox Jewish Bible, fourth edition, OJB. Copyright 2002, 2003, 2008, 2010, 2011 by Artists for Israel International. All rights reserved.

Images:

The stylised eternity symbol image used in the design of the front cover is originally by Gerd Altmann (geralt) via pixabay.com, partially redrawn by Beth Lane and Jeremy Westcott. Used by permission.

The sunrise image used in the design of the back cover is copyright Błażej Łyjak via 123RF Stock Photo. Used by permission.

CPSIA information can be obtained
at www.ICGtesting.com
Printed in the USA
LVHW042339080623
749247LV00005B/311